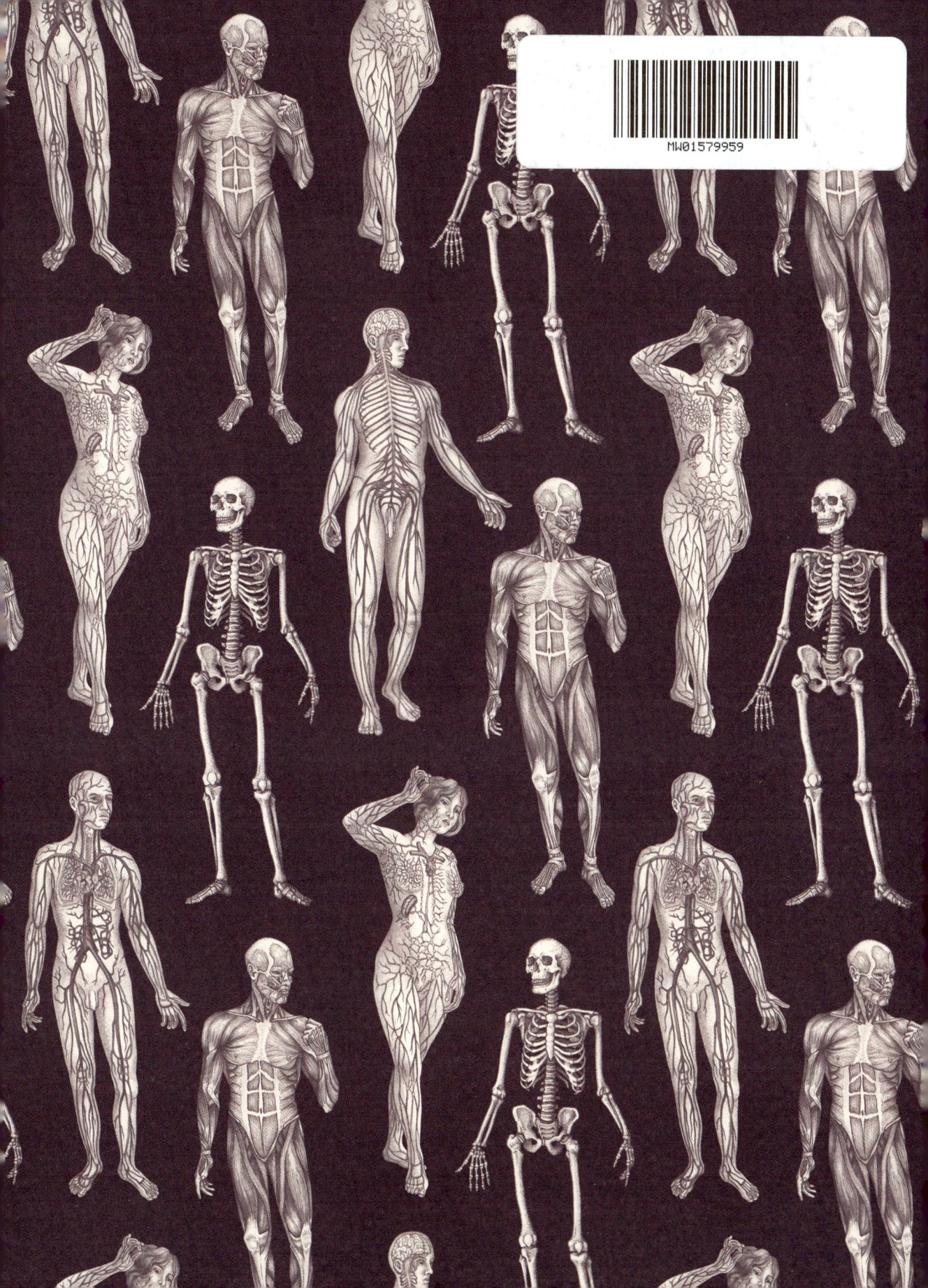

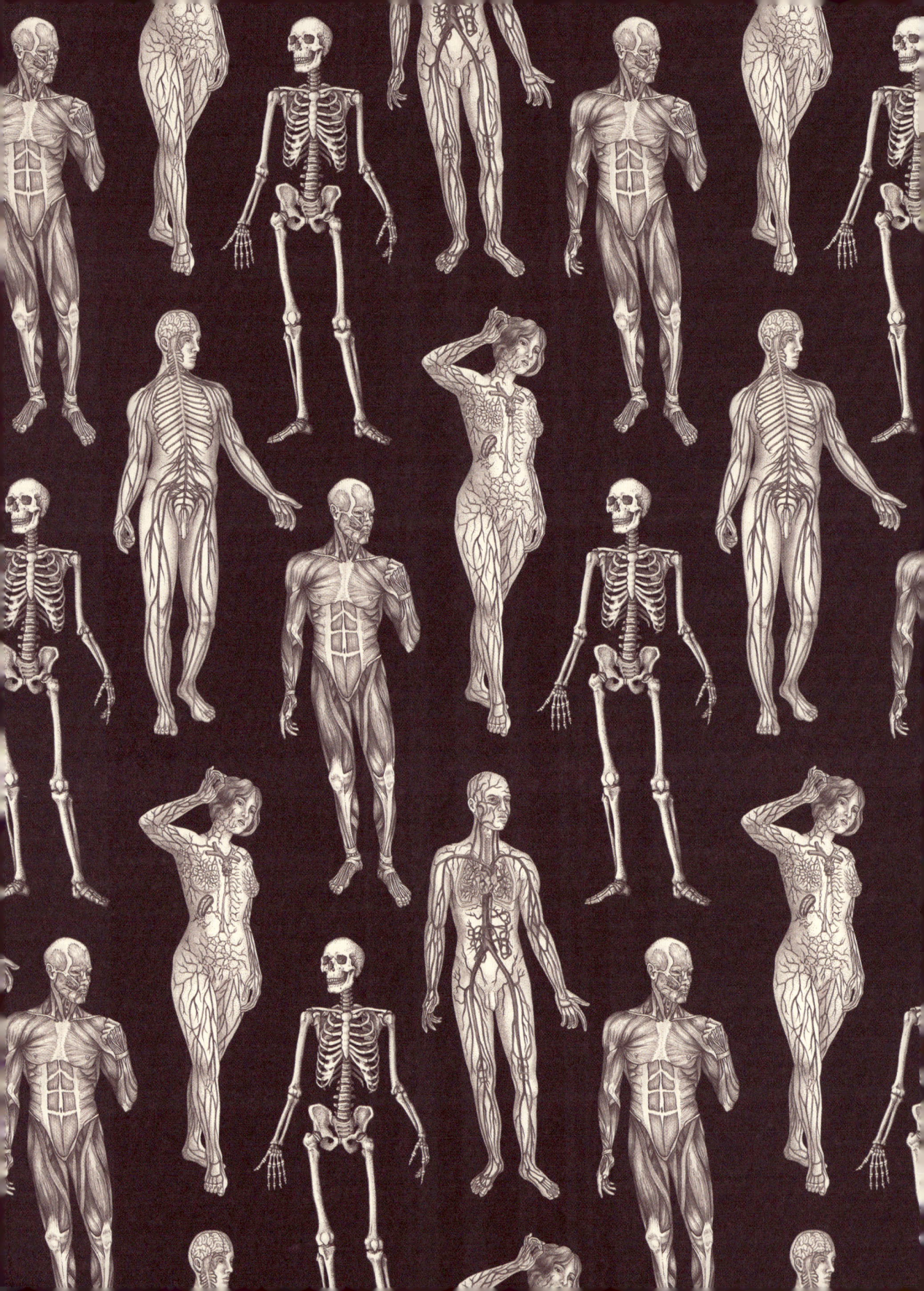

Anatomicum
Junior Edition

Illustrated by KATY WIEDEMANN
Written by JENNIFER Z PAXTON

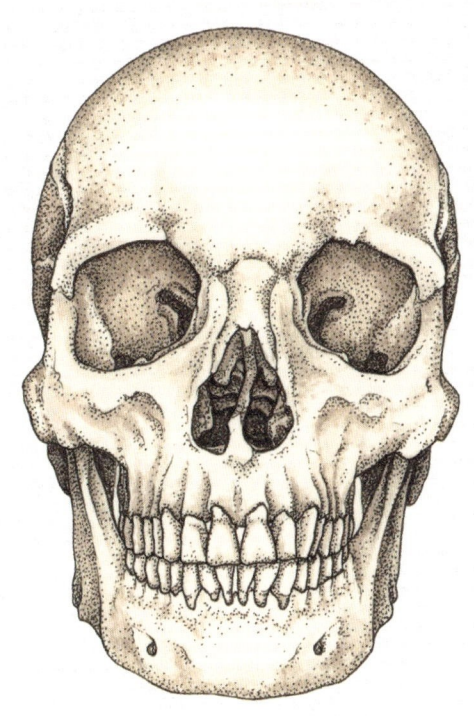

BPP

BIG PICTURE PRESS

This edition published in the UK in 2020 by Big Picture Press
First published in the UK in 2019 by Big Picture Press
an imprint of Bonnier Books UK,
The Plaza, 535 King's Road, London, SW10 0SZ
www.templarco.co.uk/big-picture-press
www.bonnierbooks.co.uk

Illustration copyright © 2019 by Katy Wiedemann
Text copyright © 2019 by Jennifer Z Paxton
Design copyright © 2020 by Big Picture Press

1 3 5 7 9 10 8 6 4 2

All rights reserved

ISBN 978-1-78741-654-3

This book was typeset in Gill Sans and Mrs Green
The illustrations were created with ink and watercolour

Original edition edited by Ruth Symons and designed by Kieran Hood
This edition edited by Lydia Watson and designed by Wendy Bartlet
Production controller: Neil Randles

Printed in Poland

1
Entrance
*Welcome to Anatomicum;
Building Blocks of the Body*

9
Gallery 1
The Musculoskeletal System
*The Skeleton; Bones; The Skull; Joints;
Connective Tissue; The Muscular System;
Muscles: Facial Expressions*

25
Gallery 2
The Circulatory & Respiratory Systems
*Cardiovascular & Respiratory Systems;
The Heart; Blood;
The Respiratory Tract & Lungs;
Immune & Lymphatic Systems*

37
Gallery 3
The Digestive & Urinary Systems
*The Digestive System; Teeth;
The Stomach; The Intestines;
The Liver; The Pancreas & Gallbladder; The
Urinary System & Kidneys*

53
Gallery 4
The Nervous System & Special Senses
*The Nervous System;
The Central Nervous System;
The Peripheral Nervous System;
The Eyes; The Ears;
The Nose & Tongue; Skin*

69
Gallery 5
The Endocrine & Reproductive Systems
*Endocrine System; Puberty;
Male Reproductive System;
Female Reproductive System;
Development of a Baby*

80
Library
Glossary

ANATOMICUM

Welcome to Anatomicum

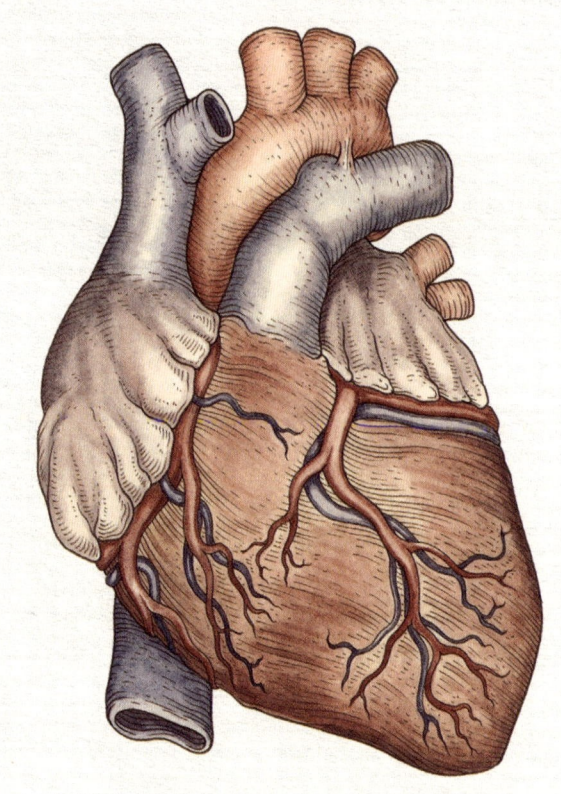

Open 24 hours a day, seven days a week, this unique museum isn't like anywhere you've ever been. As you walk its halls and corridors, you will be transported right round the human body, seeing it in vivid detail as never before.

Visit the Musculoskeletal System Gallery to discover the tissues that help us to move, or the Nervous System Gallery to examine the human brain. The exhibits will let you peer beneath the skin to look at the organs that help us breathe, and watch how food is transported and broken down.

As you explore the museum, think about how your own body is working all the time. Your heart keeps your blood pumping. Every step you take uses action from your muscles. Your eyes help you to look at each exhibit and your brain processes all of this new information. Your body is amazing!

So enter *Anatomicum* here to begin your voyage of discovery, and uncover the wonders and secrets of the human body.

Building Blocks of the Body

The human body is made up of organs, tissues, blood vessels, nerves and tiny cells. In the branch of science that we call anatomy, different parts of the body are arranged from smallest to largest, in a simple structured order.

The smallest building blocks of the body are the cells, which are too tiny to be seen by the naked eye and can only be looked at using microscopes. There are 38 trillion in the human body, each with its own special job to do. Almost every one contains DNA, the genetic information that makes us all unique.

Groups of cells join together to make body tissue, which is large enough to be seen without a microscope. Muscle tissue is like the machinery of the body. It makes up the structures that help us to move. Nervous tissue is important for communication, linking different parts of the body to the control centre of the brain. Lastly, connective tissue helps to link or support different parts of the body and hold it together.

At the next level up, different tissue types combine to make organs. These are separate parts of the body with different names and functions, such as the lungs, brain or kidneys.

Finally, several organs link up to make body systems. Each system looks after a different job, such as breathing (the respiratory system) or breaking down food (the digestive system). Although they have individual roles, the systems all work together to keep our bodies functioning properly.

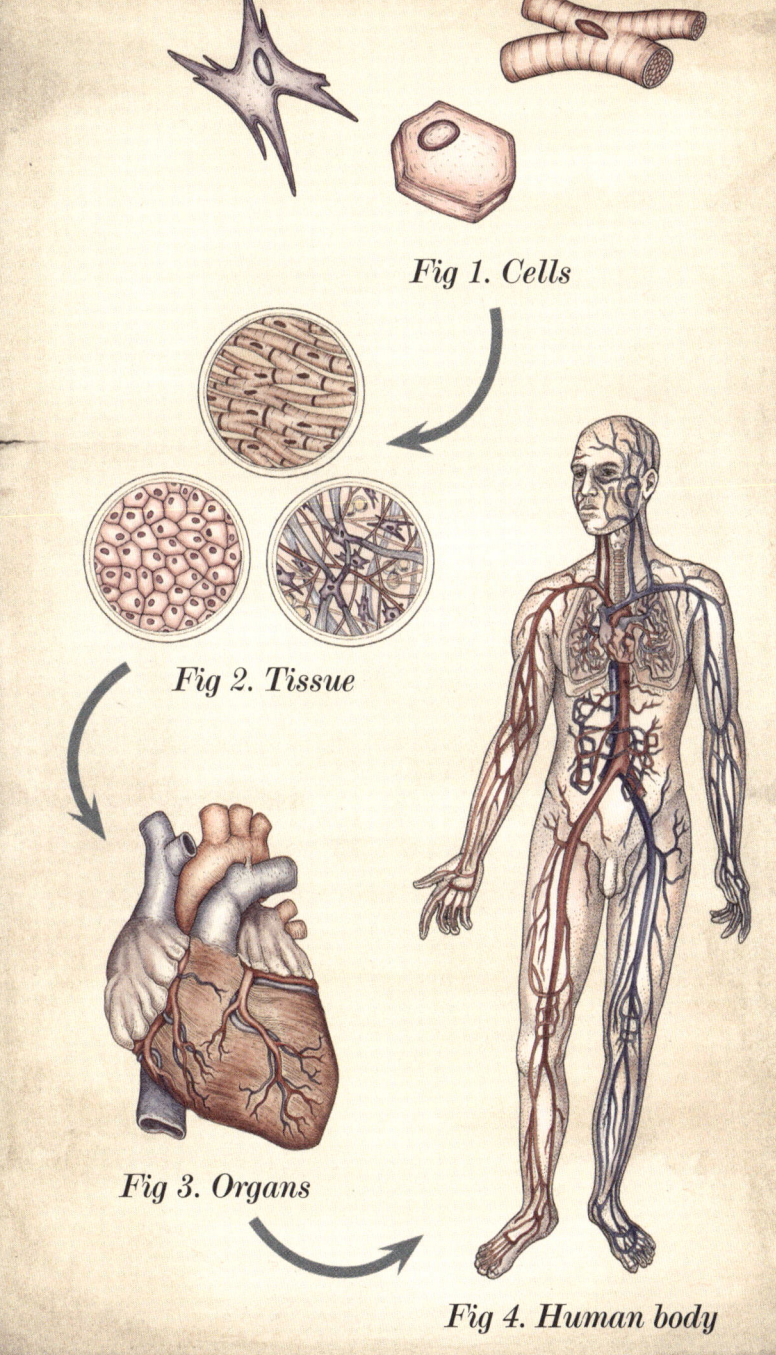

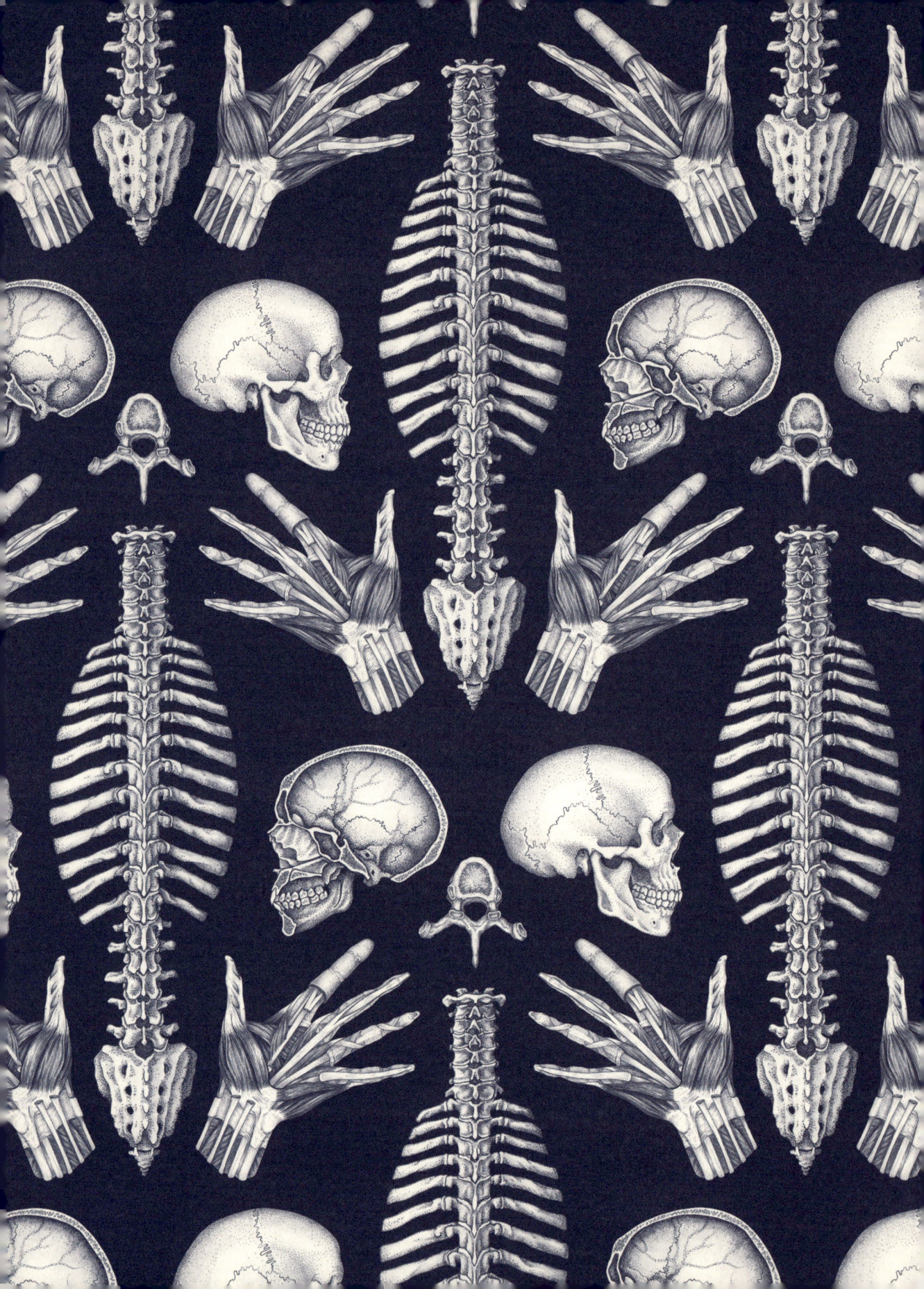

ANATOMICUM

Gallery 1

The Musculoskeletal System

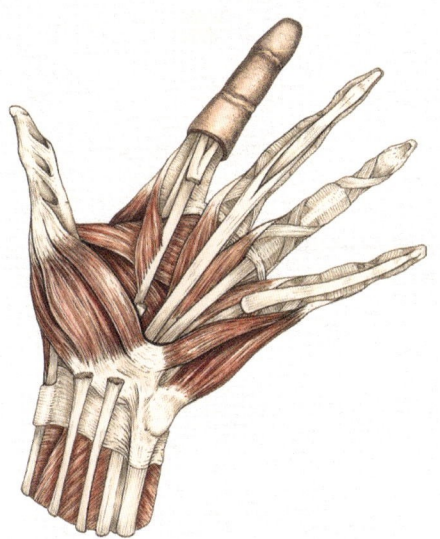

*The Skeleton; Bones;
The Skull; Joints;
Connective Tissue;
The Muscular System;
Muscles: Facial Expressions*

MUSCULOSKELETAL SYSTEM

The Skeleton

The skeleton provides the frame for the entire human body. It gives us our overall shape, supports the muscles, protects the organs and makes new blood cells. It is made up of 206 bones, which link together at areas called joints. These keep the bones of the skeleton fixed to each other and also allow us to move. Anatomists split the skeleton into two parts, axial and appendicular.

The axial skeleton includes all the bones of the head and the torso, supporting the upper body and protecting the inner organs. It also includes the vertebral column (spine), a long row of 33 bones called vertebrae that surround the delicate spinal cord. Together, the vertebrae make a curved, flexible pillar, which can bend forwards, backwards or side-to-side. At the very top of the spine, the vertebrae connect to and support the skull and the brain.

The appendicular skeleton is made up of the bones in the limbs and pelvis. The bones of the upper limbs – the arm, forearm, wrist and hand – are strong and supple and help with tasks like threading a needle and batting a ball. The bones of the lower limbs – the thigh, leg, ankle and foot – are mainly there to support our weight as we walk, stand or run. Key to this is the longest and strongest bone in the human body: the femur or thigh bone.

Key to plate

1: Skeleton, front view
a) Cranium (skull bones)
b) Clavicle (collar bone)
c) Sternum (breast bone)
d) Humerus (arm bone)
e) Ribs
f) Pelvis (hip bones)
g) Ulna (inner forearm bone)
h) Radius (outer forearm bone)
i) Femur (thigh bone)
j) Patella (knee cap)
k) Tibia (inner leg bone)
l) Fibula (outer leg bone)
m) Tarsals (ankle bones)
n) Metatarsals (foot bones)

2: Skeleton, back view
a) Vertebral column (spine or backbone)
b) Scapula (shoulder blade)
c) Sacrum (fused bones at base of spine)
d) Coccyx (tail bone)

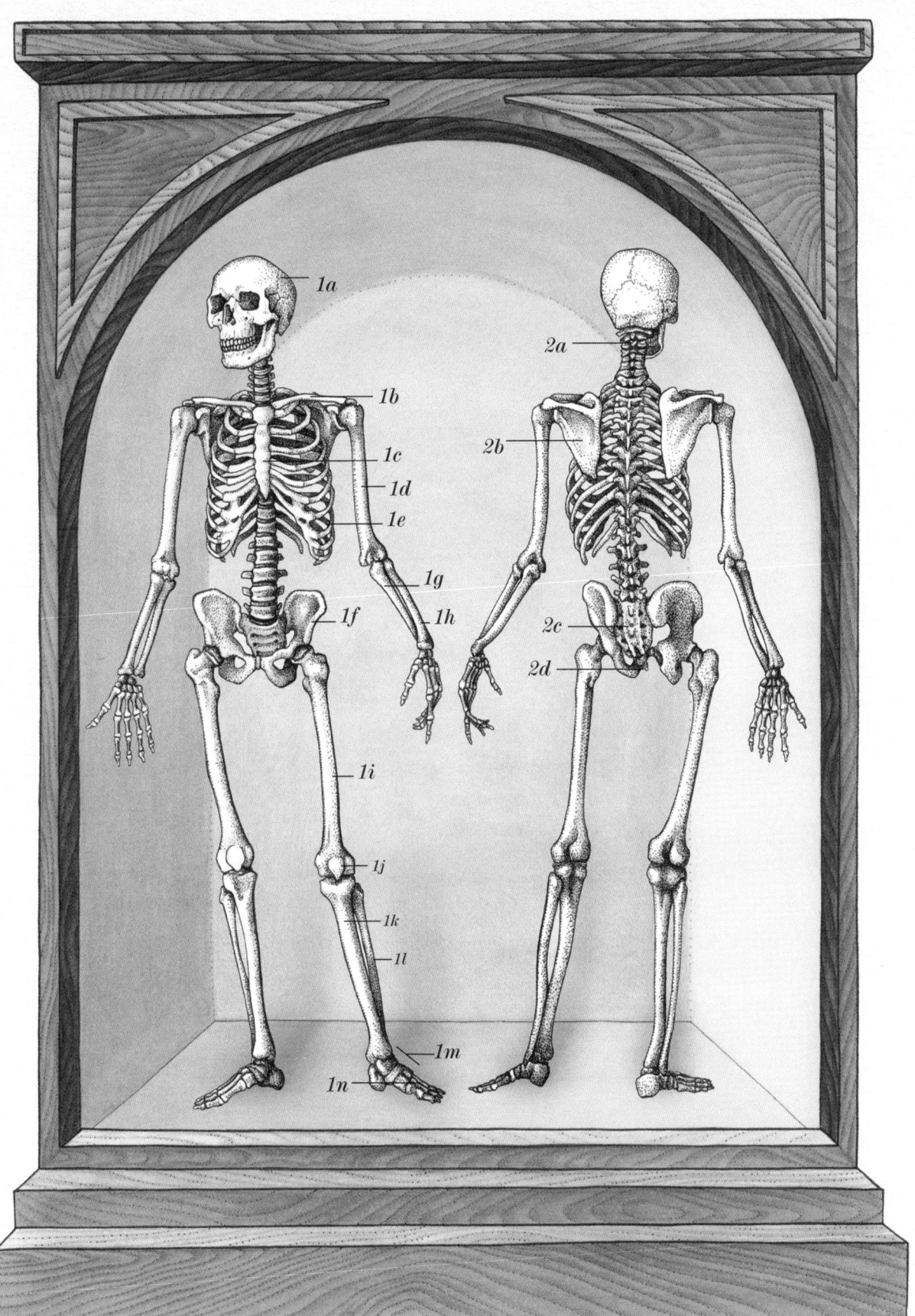

> MUSCULOSKELETAL SYSTEM

Bones

There are five types of bone: long, short, flat, sesamoid and irregular. Long bones like the femur support the body's weight. Short bones, such as those in the wrist, support the joints. Flat bones, such as those in the skull, protect the body's organs. Sesamoid bones, such as those in the kneecap, are small, round bones found inside connective tissue called tendons (see page 18). All other kinds are irregular bones. These have complicated shapes made for specific jobs, like the bones of the vertebrae.

All bones are made from calcium (a mineral that makes bones sturdy) and collagen (a protein that makes them a little springy). This combination means that bones are strong and won't snap under pressure.

Scientists know that bones are always growing. We are born with over 300 bones, but some of these fuse together to make the 206 bones of the adult skeleton. Bones can repair themselves, too. There is a rich blood supply that means nutrients go straight to the damaged area of the bone. That's why most fractures take just six weeks to heal. Bones also respond to our lifestyle, especially to exercise. After lots of movement, more bone is produced. Less movement – like when you're ill – makes bones weaker.

--- *Key to plate* ---

1: **Vertebra**
a) Single vertebra (viewed from above): Vertebrae are irregular bones that support the upper body. The spinal cord runs through a hole in the middle.
b) Vertebral column (spine) and ribs: The spine is made up of 33 individual vertebrae. Ribs form joints with 12 of them to make 24 ribs in total.

2: **Knee bones**
Patella (knee cap): This is an example of a sesamoid bone.

3: **Foot bones, top view**
There are 26 foot bones altogether, in various shapes and sizes. The tarsal bones that make up the ankle are short bones that fit together.

4: **Sternum, front view**
The sternum (breast bone) is a flat bone at the front of the ribcage. It protects the delicate heart and lungs underneath it.

5: **Femur, back view**
The rounded ball at the top of this long bone is the femoral head, which forms part of the hip joint.

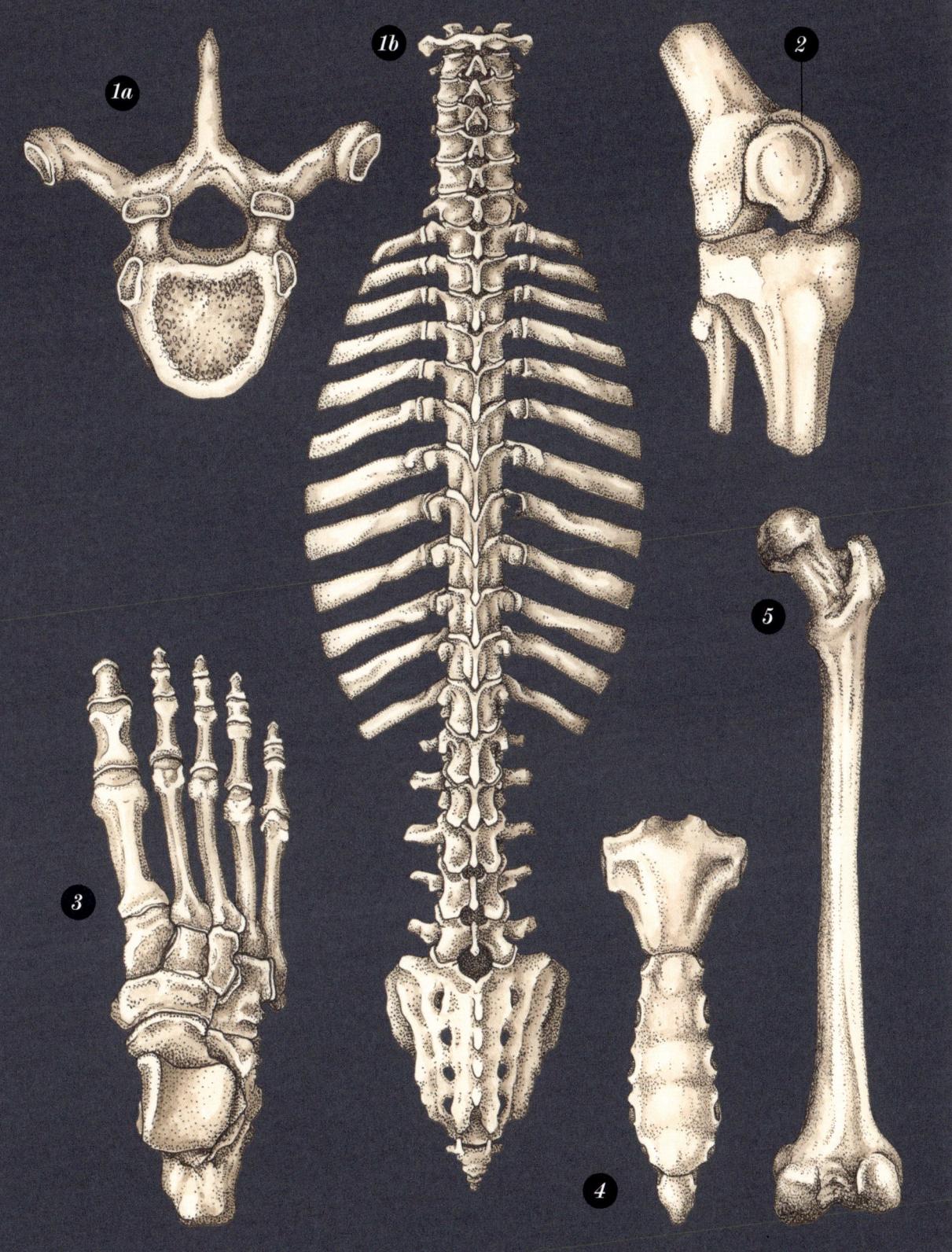

> MUSCULOSKELETAL SYSTEM

The Skull

Underneath the skin and muscles of our head lies the skull, a protective home for the brain and sensory organs (the eyes, ears, nose and tongue). It is formed of 22 individual bones. The top part, or vault, is formed of eight bones and acts like a helmet, shielding the delicate brain inside from injury. The other 14 bones provide shape for the face and jaw. Only one of these, the mandible, or jawbone, can move. This bone is joined to the skull by a hinge joint (see page 16), which lets us open and close the jaw during chewing and talking.

Most of the skull bones have air-filled spaces inside them called sinuses. These make the skull lighter and make our voices clearer by allowing air to vibrate within them. There are also holes called foramina running right through the skull bones. These let the brain connect with other parts of the body via nerves, and allow blood vessels to pass to and from the brain and face.

You might notice that the ears and nose aren't visible. This is because the structure of the nose and ear is made from cartilage. This material is softer and decays more quickly than bone.

After a person dies, their skull might give us clues about them. We can guess the age, sex and ethnicity by studying the skull's size and features. Some scientists study bones to find out about ancient cultures, while others study bones to uncover clues about the cause of death in criminal cases.

Key to plate

1: **Adult skull**
a) From the front
b) From the back
c) From the base (without jaw): The large central hole in the base of the skull is called the foramen magnum. This is where the spinal cord comes out of the skull to travel down the vertebral column.
d) From the side
e) Cross-section from the side: The space inside the skull where the brain sits is called the cranial fossa.

2: **Newborn skull**
The bones of an adult skull are fused together and cannot move, but in babies, these joints are made of more flexible material. These 'soft spots' mean the skull can cope with the rapid growth of a baby's brain, from only about 350g at birth to nearly 600g, in the first three months.
a) From the top: The diamond-shaped area is the 'soft spot'.
b) From the front: Infant skulls have a bigger forehead and a smaller jaw than adults' skulls.
c) From the side: Note the large forehead and small jaw.

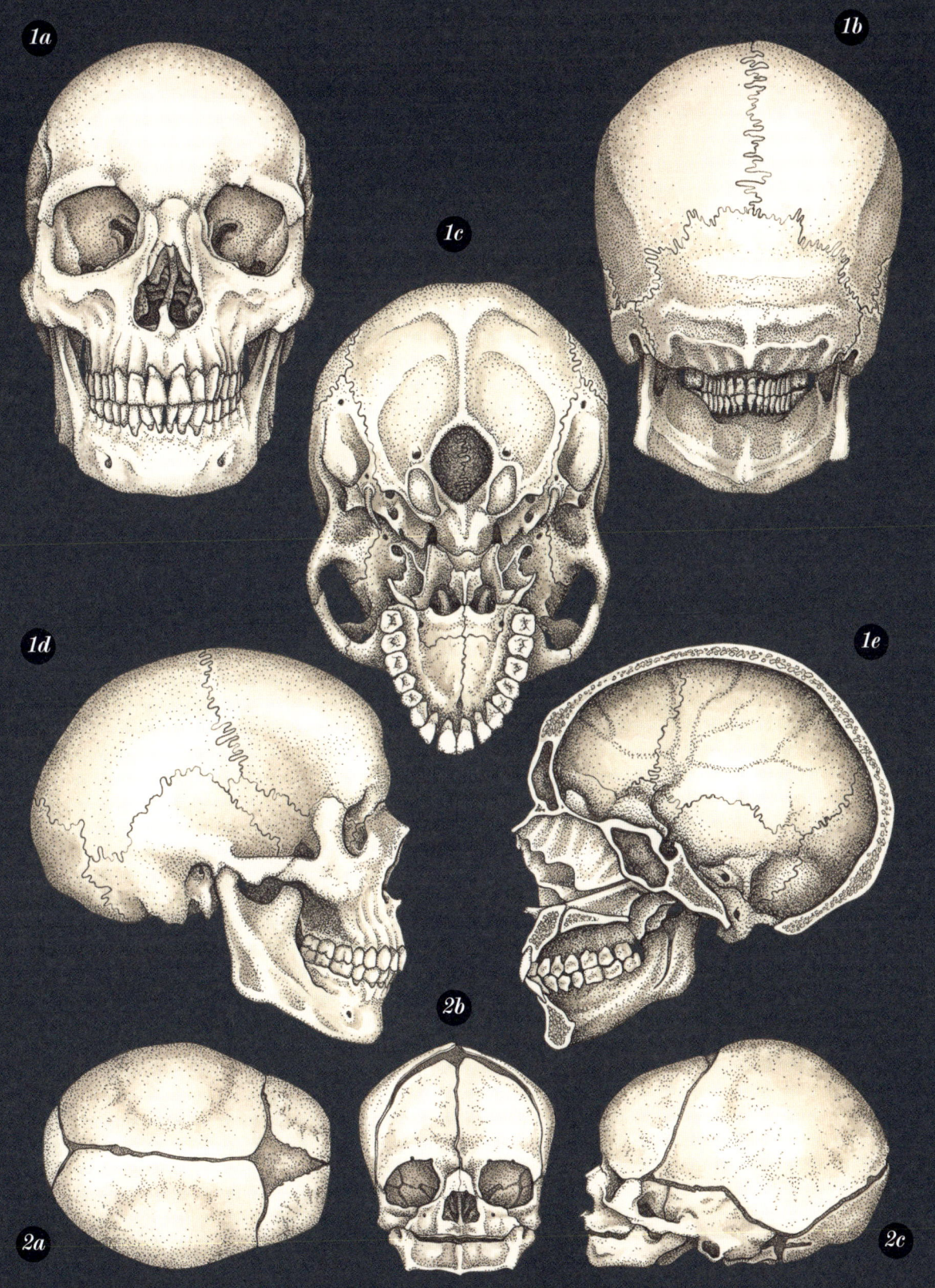

> MUSCULOSKELETAL SYSTEM

Joints

Joints are where two or more bones link together. In total there are over 300 joints in the body, connecting most bones to at least one more. Joints are often thought of as the parts of the skeleton that move, but there are actually three different types. Some can move, but others can't.

Fibrous or immovable joints are one type of joint that can't move. They hold bones together and keep them stable. For example, the bones of the adult skull come together at fibrous joints called sutures.

Cartilaginous joints are slightly more flexible. Here, a layer of soft tissue called cartilage sits between the bones and joins them together. These joints allow for a little movement, so the bones can shift position slightly.

The most common type of joints are the movable, or synovial, joints, such as those in the hip or knee. The ends of the bones are covered in a layer of soft tissue called hyaline cartilage (see page 18), which helps to reduce friction as the bones slide past each other. The bones are held together by tough bands of tissue called ligaments, while a special structure called a joint capsule wraps around the joint to help keep it together. This capsule contains a slippery liquid called synovial fluid, which keeps the joint working smoothly.

―――――――――― *Key to plate* ――――――――――

1: **Pivot joint**
In pivot joints, one bone rotates around another. The pivot joint between the first two vertebrae is used to turn the head from side to side.

2: **Ball-and-socket joint**
In joints like the one in the shoulder, the 'ball' of one bone fits into a 'socket' on the next bone. It allows movement in lots of different directions.

3: **Hinge joint**
Hinge joints allow movement in one direction only. They act like door hinges, allowing joins between bones to bend, but not rotate. Major hinge joints of the body are at the elbows, knees and ankles.

4: **Condyloid joint**
These are found in places like the wrist, where one bone is rounded and fits into a hollow on the bone next to it.

5: **Saddle joint**
These joints, like the one aat the base of the thumb, look like a saddle on top of another bone. They allow side-to-side and bending movement.

6: **Planar or gliding joint**
These occur in places like the tarsal bones, where bones lie flat against each other. They allow bones to slide from side to side or up and down.

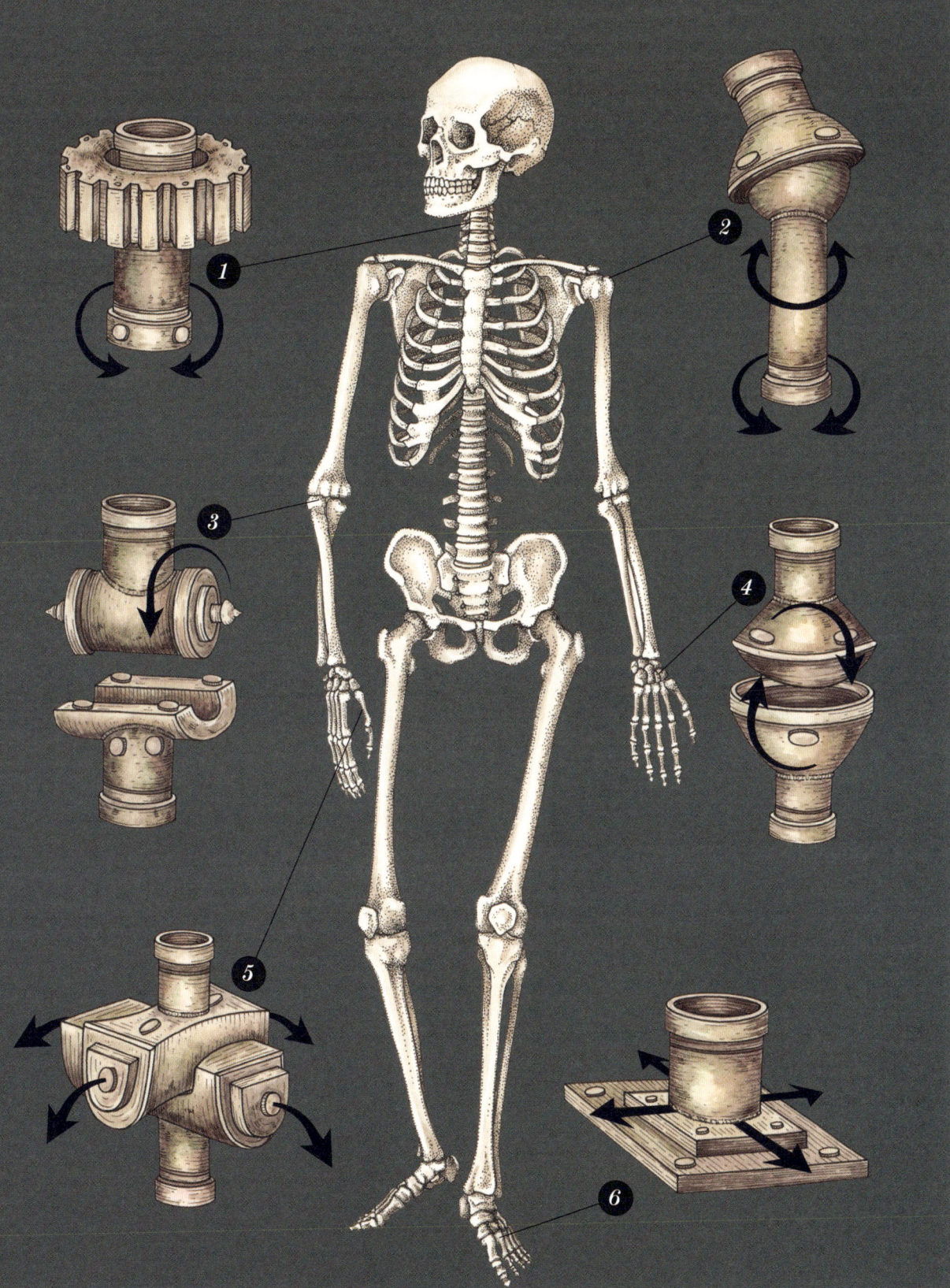

MUSCULOSKELETAL SYSTEM

Connective Tissue

As well as bones and muscles, there are also connective tissues in the skeletal system that join it all together. Connective tissues like tendons, ligaments and cartilage connect, support and protect the entire skeleton.

Tendons are thick straps of tissue linking muscle to bone, made from a protein called collagen. When a muscle contracts (squeezes), it gets shorter, which pulls on the tendon so that it moves the bone. Ligaments are similar, but instead of connecting muscle to bone, they connect bone to bone. They help to keep joints stable in places where the bones do not slot together very well, like the knee. The knee joint has several ligaments to make it more sturdy.

Cartilage is a soft, flexible substance found all over the body, in three different types. Hyaline cartilage acts as a shock absorber at joints and reduces friction between bones. Fibrocartilage is found in soft, squashy discs between the vertebrae of the spine and in the bones of the knee joint. Lastly, elastic cartilage is a special bouncy tissue that forms the shape of the outer ear.

―――― *Key to plate* ――――

1: Knee joint and leg, front and side view (no muscles)
a) Quadriceps tendon: Joins the quadriceps muscle to the tibia (shin bone) and holds the patella (knee cap).
b) Patella
c) Fibular collateral ligament: Connects the femur (thigh bone) to the fibula (outer leg bone).
d) Cartilage: Sits on the surface of bones where they meet in the skeleton and reduces friction.
e) The anterior and posterior cruciate ligaments: Sit inside the knee joint and join the femur and tibia together.
f) The patellar ligament: Joins the patella to the tibia.
g) Ligaments of the ankle joint: Help to hold the ankle bones together for stability.

2: Knee joint and leg, back view (with muscles)
a) Calf muscle
b) Achilles tendon: The largest and strongest tendon in the body, joining the calf muscle to the heel bone. It is named after the ancient Greek warrior Achilles, whose only weak spot was his ankle.
c) Heel bone

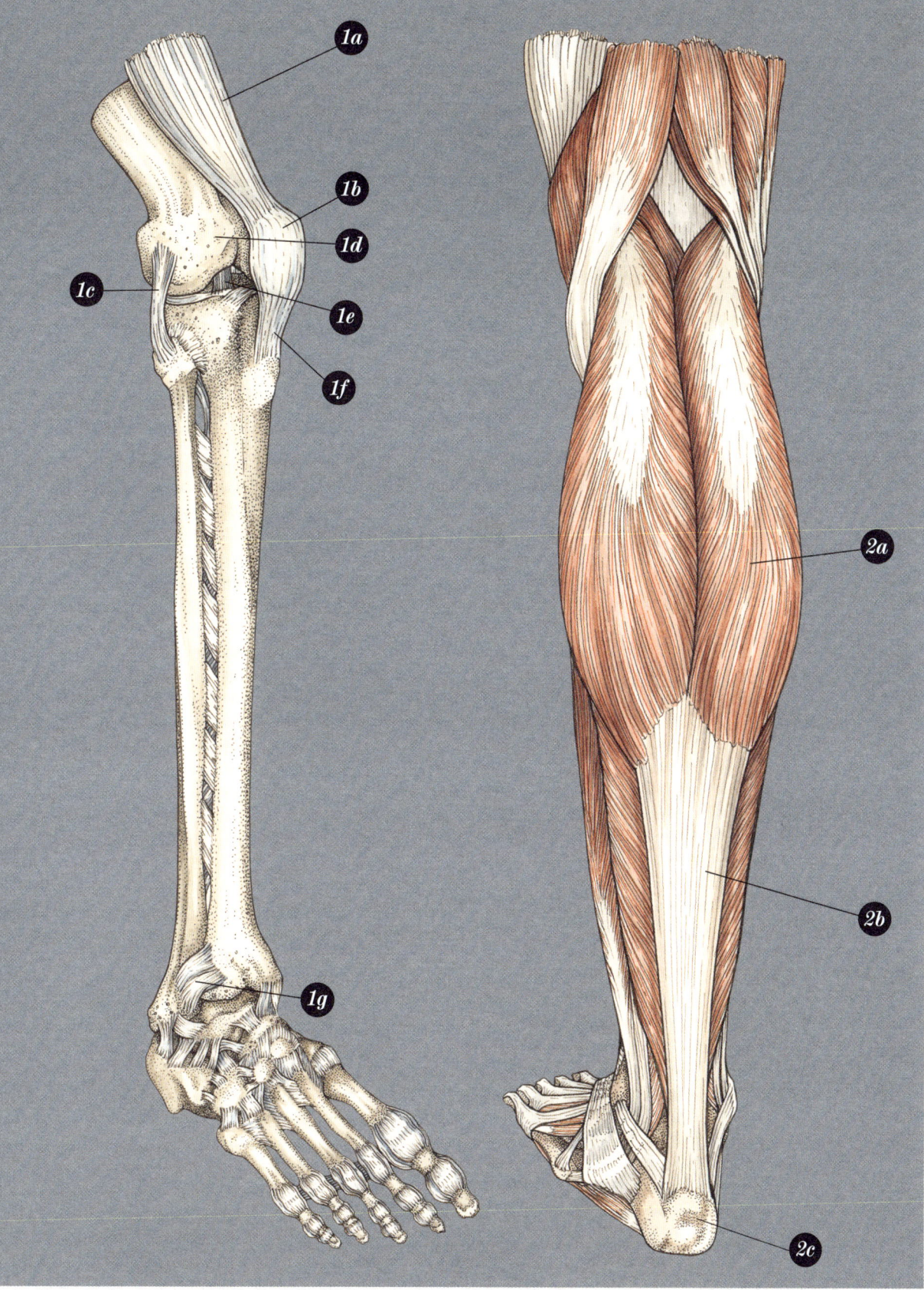

MUSCULOSKELETAL SYSTEM

The Muscular System

From the first steps of a baby to the sprint of an Olympic runner, the muscular system makes every possible type of movement happen.

Muscle tissue is found all through the body in three types – skeletal, cardiac and smooth – and makes the body move by contraction. When skeletal muscle contracts, it gets shorter, pulling on the bones it's attached to. This moves them into a new position. These muscles can only pull in one direction, so they usually work in pairs. After one muscle contracts to bend a joint, another muscle contracts to straighten it out again. Skeletal muscle gives the body its shape, and is thought to add up to 40 per cent of an adult's total body weight.

As well as moving the skeleton, the muscular system has other important jobs to do. Cardiac muscle pumps blood around the body, smooth muscle moves food through the digestive tract, and skeletal muscle communicates by making facial expressions. Muscles even help us keep warm – in fact, muscle contractions produce around 70 per cent of our total body heat.

Key to plate

1: Skeletal muscles, back view
There are over 600 named skeletal muscles in the body. Their names follow rules based on the action, shape, size or location of the muscle. *Flexor* and *extensor* tell you that the muscle is either a bending muscle (*flexor*) or a muscle that straightens at the joint (*extensor*). Scientific terms also tell you the size of muscles: maximus (large); minimus (small); longus (long); and brevis (short). The word 'muscle' itself comes from the Latin for 'little mouse'. This might be because the muscle belly (the central part that bulges) and tendon (that attaches it to the bone) resemble a mouse and its tail.
a) Trapezius
b) Latissimus dorsi
c) Gluteus maximus
d) Hamstrings
e) Calf muscle
f) Triceps brachii
g) Deltoid

2: Skeletal muscles, front view
a) Pectoralis major
b) Biceps brachii
c) Rectus abdominus
d) Quadriceps
e) Tibialis anterior

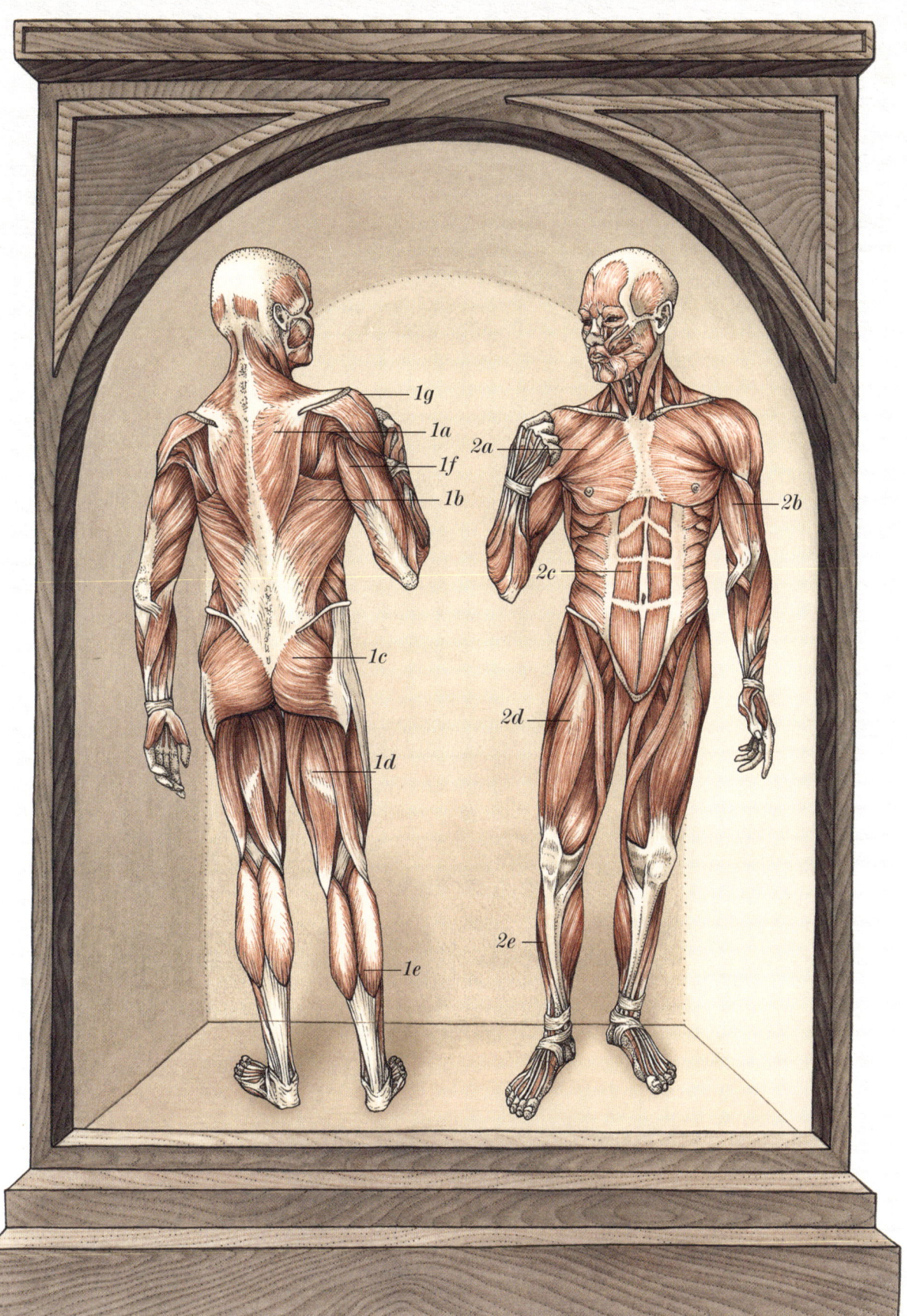

> MUSCULOSKELETAL SYSTEM

Muscles: Facial Expressions

You can often tell how someone is feeling by the expression on their face. Are they happy, sad, angry or worried? Even though we communicate with each other by speaking, we also communicate through body language, especially facial expressions. We have over 40 muscles under the skin of our face, connecting to the bones of the skull. The muscles and bones work together to produce over 10,000 facial expressions.

Some facial muscles, such as the muscles surrounding the eyes and mouth, have a specific role. The *orbicularis oris* is around the mouth and known as the 'kissing muscle'. It is used to close and stick out the lips. The *depressor anguli oris* pulls the mouth downwards, creating the 'sad face' expression. The muscle used to show surprise is the *frontalis* muscle on the forehead – it pulls the eyebrows upwards and wrinkles the forehead.

We use more muscles when we frown than when we smile. Real smiles of happiness use muscles around the eyes, as well as the mouth, that we can't control. This is how we tell the difference between a fake smile and a real one!

Key to plate

1: Muscles of facial expression
a) Frontalis
b) Temporalis
c) Orbicularis oculi
d) Nasalis
e) Orbicularis oris
f) Levator labii superioris
g) Zygomaticus *major* and *minor*
h) Depressor anguli oris
i) Mentalis

2: Kissing muscles
The *orbicularis oris* muscle closes and pushes out the lips.

3: Muscles of smiling and winking
Zygomaticus major pulls the corners of the mouth up to smile. When you wink, the *orbicularis oculi* muscle closes the eyelid. It also moves involuntarily when you smile.

4: Muscles of sadness
Depressor anguli oris pulls the corners of the mouth down.

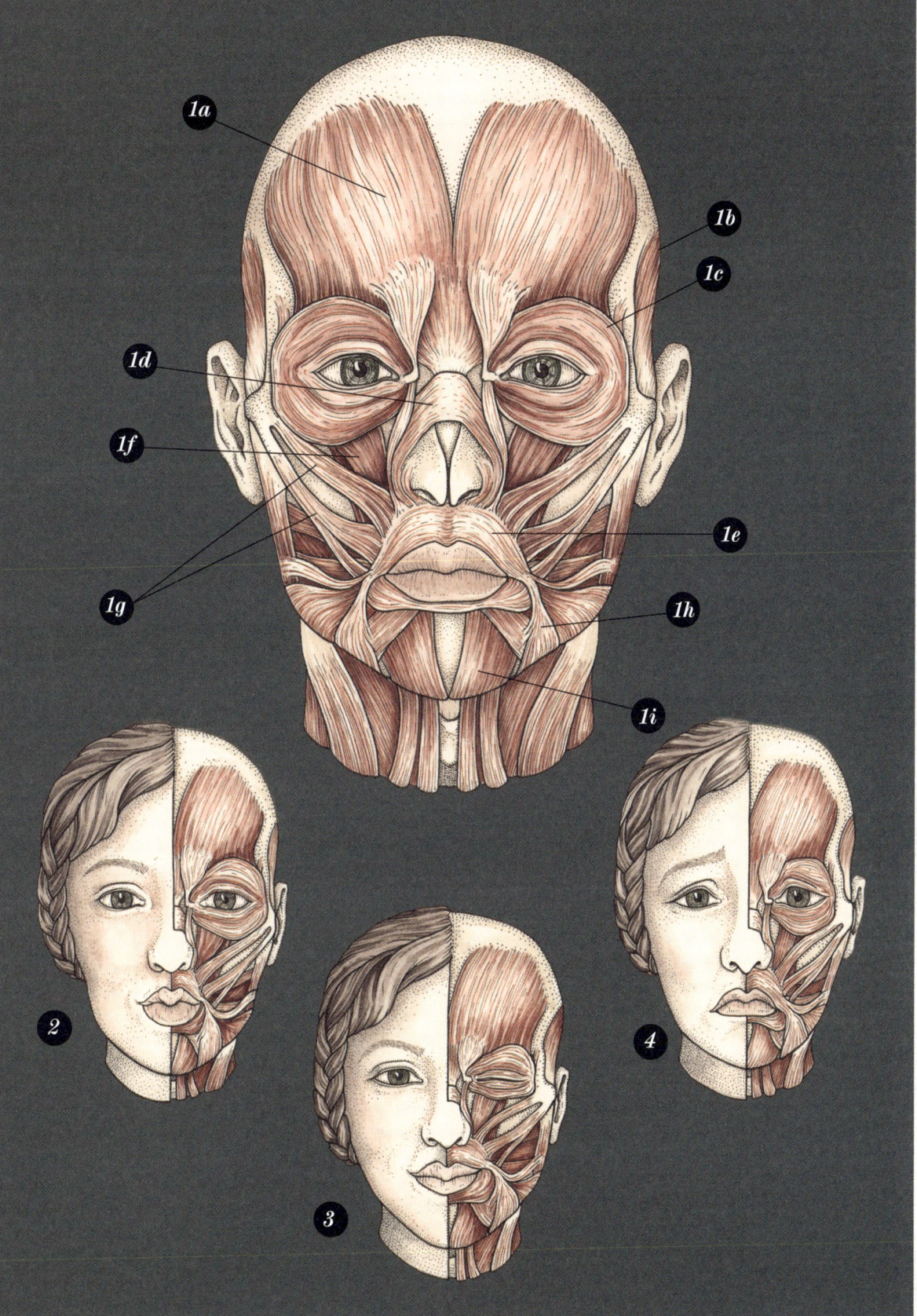

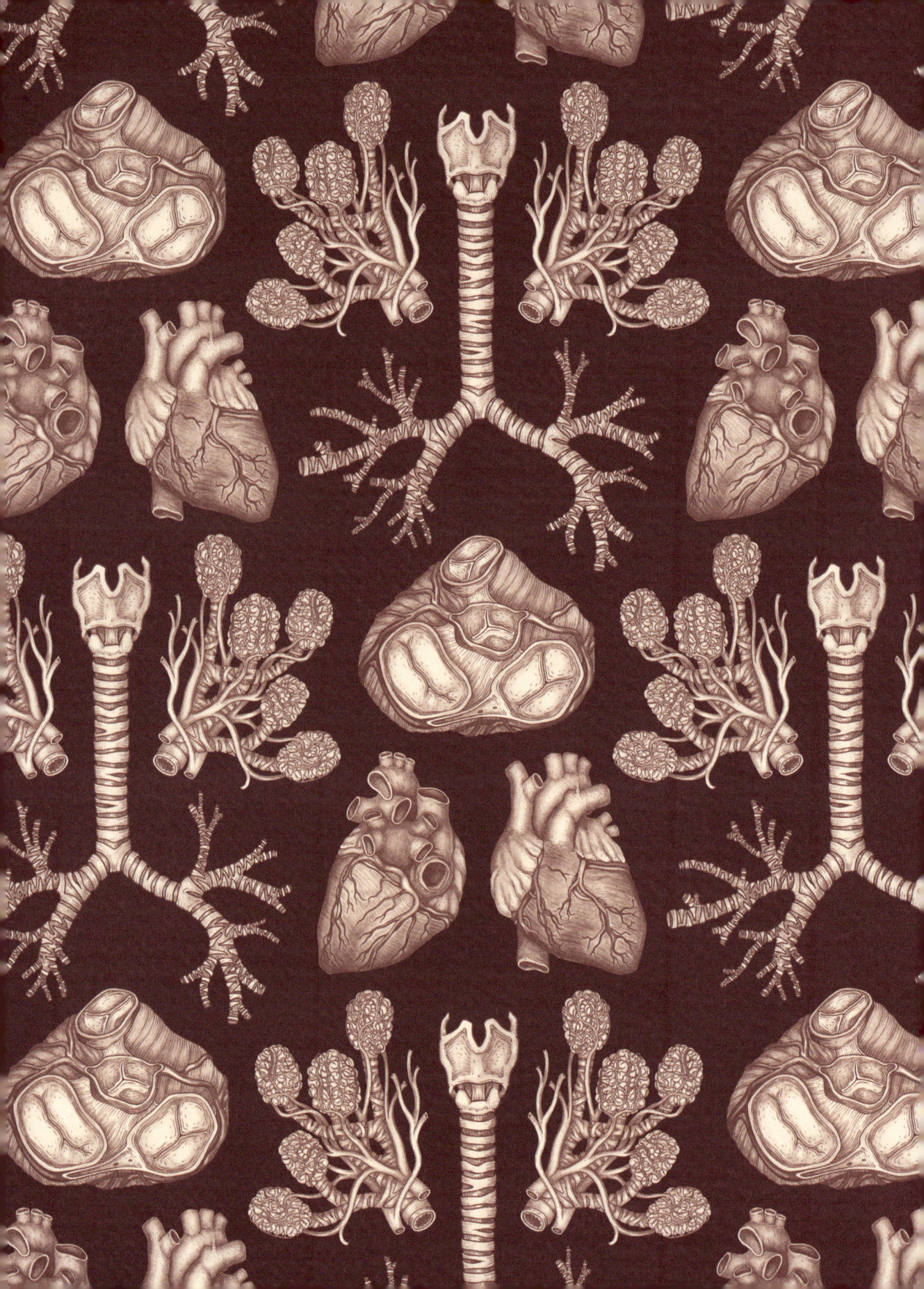

ANATOMICUM

Gallery 2

The Circulatory & Respiratory Systems

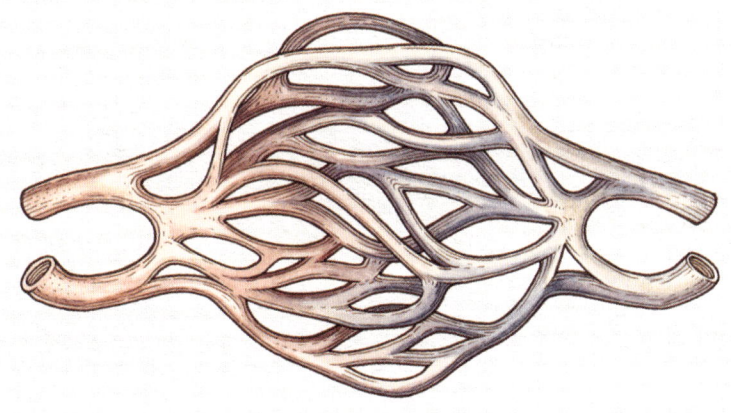

Cardiovascular & Respiratory Systems;
The Heart; Blood;
The Lungs & Respiratory Tract;
Immune & Lymphatic Systems

CIRCULATORY &
RESPIRATORY SYSTEMS

Cardiovascular and Respiratory Systems

Every cell in the body needs oxygen to turn into energy – a process called respiration. When cells release energy, they also produce a gas called carbon dioxide, which the body needs to get rid of. Inhaling oxygen and exhaling carbon dioxide is the task of the respiratory system. It works together with the cardiovascular system, which pumps blood around the body to transport oxygen and remove waste carbon dioxide.

To reach the body's cells, oxygen travels through both systems. First, air is breathed in through the nose and mouth and goes through the trachea (windpipe) into the lungs. Here, the oxygen in the air enters the cardiovascular system through the bloodstream. The oxygenated blood travels right round the body through a network of tubes called blood vessels (see page 30), powered by the beating of the heart. It delivers oxygen to each cell and carries away carbon dioxide. Deoxygenated blood travels back to the lungs and the respiratory system and carbon dioxide is breathed out.

―――――――――――― *Key to plate* ――――――――――――

1: **Heart**

2: **Arterial system**
The collection of blood vessels, called arteries, that transports blood away from the heart and to the body tissues.
a) Subclavian artery
b) Axillary artery
c) Abdominal aorta
d) Brachial artery

e) Radial artery
f) Common iliac artery
g) External iliac artery
h) Ulnar artery
i) Femoral artery
j) Popliteal artery

3: **Venous system**
The collection of blood vessels, called veins, that transports blood to the heart.

a) Subclavian vein
b) Inferior vena cava
c) Common iliac vein
d) Femoral vein
e) Popliteal vein

4: **Lungs**

5: **Trachea (windpipe)**

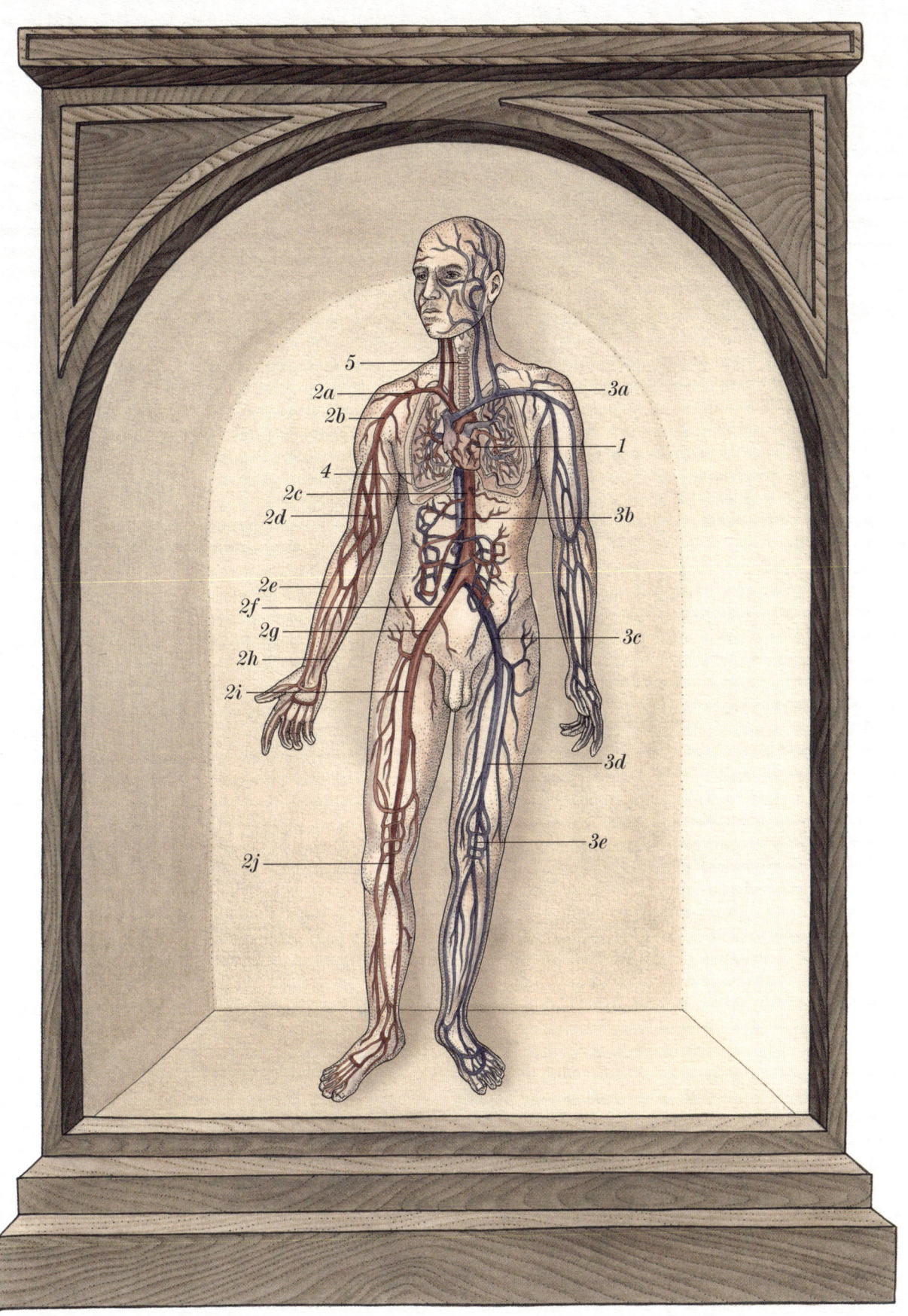

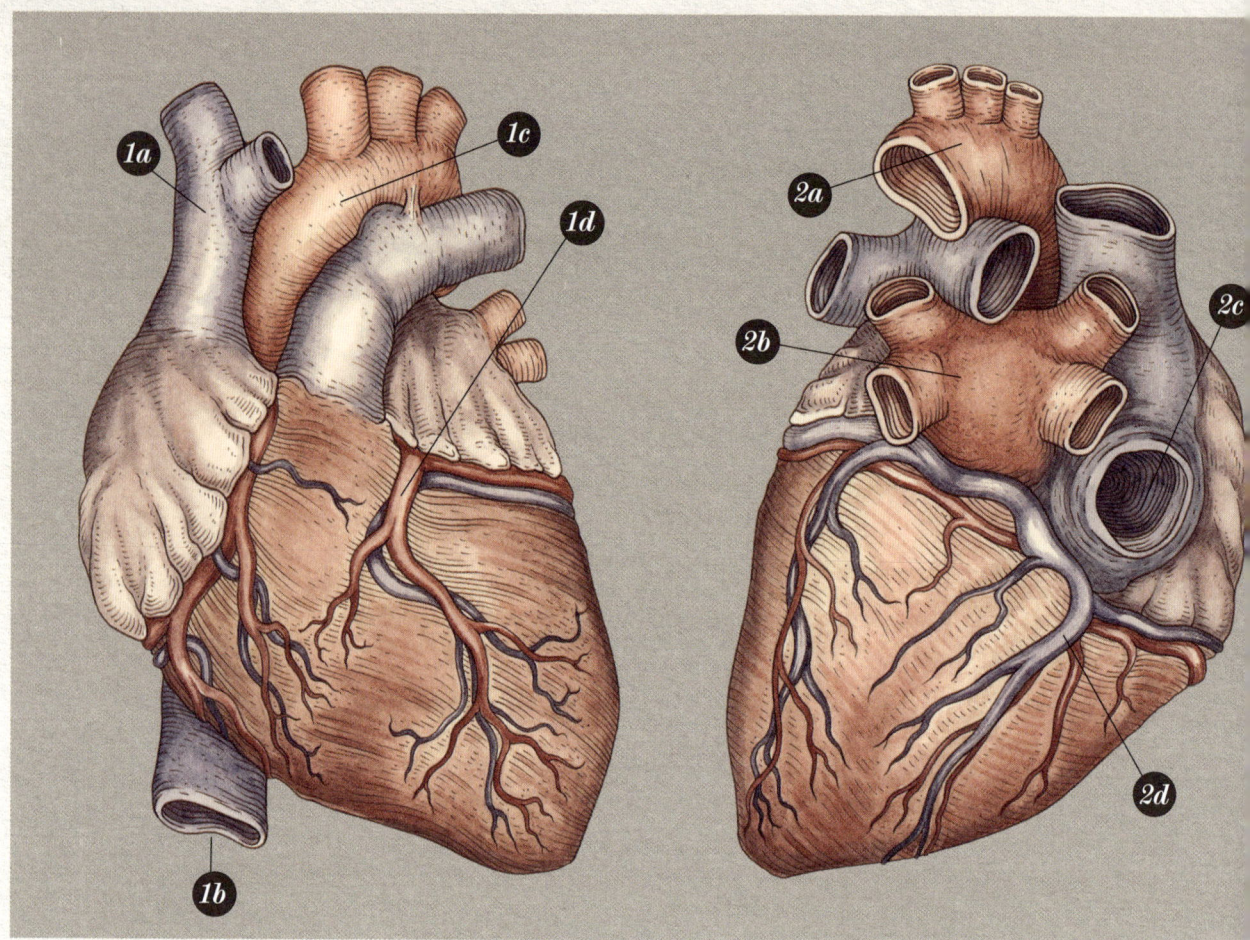

CIRCULATORY & RESPIRATORY SYSTEMS

The Heart

The heart is the hardest working muscle in the body, beating over 100,000 times a day. It is only about the size of a fist and acts like two pumps. The right-hand side pumps blood towards the lungs, where it picks up oxygen. Oxygenated blood returns to the to heart and the left-hand side pumps it on to the rest of the body. A thick wall called the septum divides the right and left sides and keeps the blood separate.

The pumping action of the heart is produced by cardiac muscle in its walls, which contracts to push blood from one side to the other. There are four chambers (areas) of the heart, which are split into two ventricles at the bottom and two atria at the top.

With each heartbeat, the two atria contract to push the blood inside

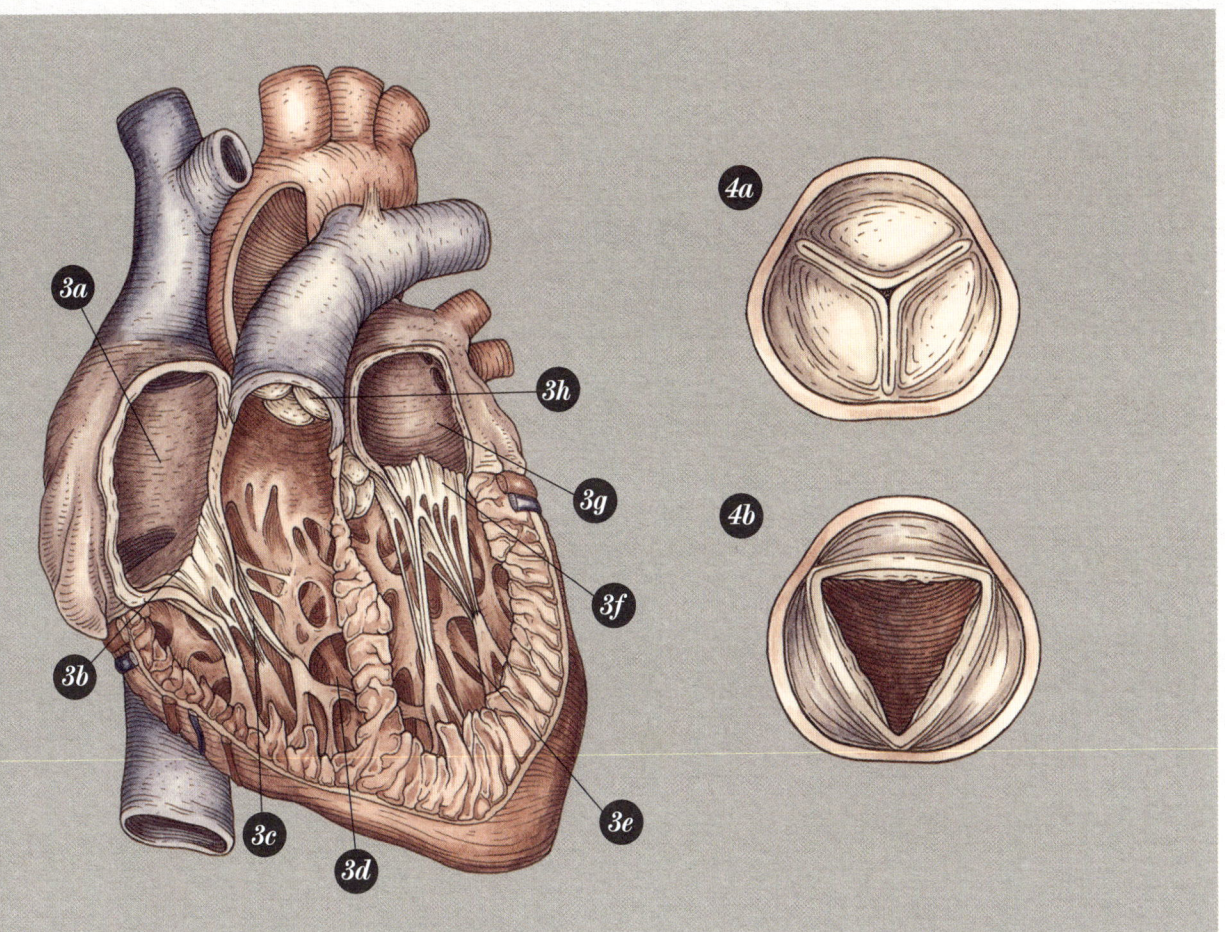

them down into the ventricles. Then the ventricles contract, which pushes the blood out of the heart and on to other parts of the body. The heart muscles relax and the chambers refill with blood, ready for the next contraction. One complete cycle of this pattern, or heartbeat, takes less than a second to occur.

--- Key to plate ---

1: **Heart, front view**
a) Superior vena cava
b) Inferior vena cava
c) Arch of aorta
d) Cardiac blood vessels supplying the wall of the heart

2: **Heart, back view**
a) Arch of aorta
b) Left atrium
c) Entrance to right atrium via inferior vena cava
d) Cardiac vessels draining the wall of the heart

3: **Internal structure of the heart, front view**
a) Right atrium
b) Tricuspid valve
c) Chordae tendinae (heart strings)
d) Right ventricle
e) Left ventricle
f) Mitral (bicuspid) valve
g) Left atrium
h) Pulmonary valve

4: **Heart valves**
These control the flow of blood in and out of the heart.
a) Closed
b) Open

Blood

Blood is made up of billions of cells. Ninety-nine per cent of these are red blood cells, which carry oxygen around the body, and 0.2 per cent are white blood cells, which attack infection and take away damaged cells. The final 0.8 per cent of blood cells are platelets, which help stop bleeding. Platelets clot the blood to make it thick and sticky, forming a protective scab over wounds.

A huge network of tubes called blood vessels carries blood to every part of our body. Within this network there are different types of blood vessel doing different jobs. Arteries carry blood away from the heart, veins carry blood towards the heart and capillaries join the two together.

All blood vessels have walls made of muscle. Arteries have the thickest and strongest walls, as they carry high-pressure blood away from the heart. They divide like tree branches into arterioles, which then turn into capillaries, the narrowest type of blood vessel. Once blood has travelled through the capillaries, it flows into tiny veins called venules. Veins have much thinner walls than arteries because the blood they carry is not travelling with so much force.

--- *Key to plate* ---

1: **Artery**
Arteries transport blood away from the heart. They branch into smaller arterioles before joining capillaries.

2: **Capillary bed**
Tiny blood vessels called capillaries form the capillary bed, where gas and nutrient exchange takes place.

3: **Vein**
These muscular tubes have thinner, stretchier walls than arteries and are much wider. They contain valves that stop blood flowing back on itself as it makes its journey back to the heart.

4: **Blood composition**
a) Plasma: A watery mixture of hormones and nutrients.
b) Red blood cells: Flat, disc-shaped cells that carry oxygen around the body.
c) White blood cells: These are part of the immune system and help the body to fight infection.
d) Platelets: Tiny cells which rush to wounds and form scabs to stop blood from escaping the body.

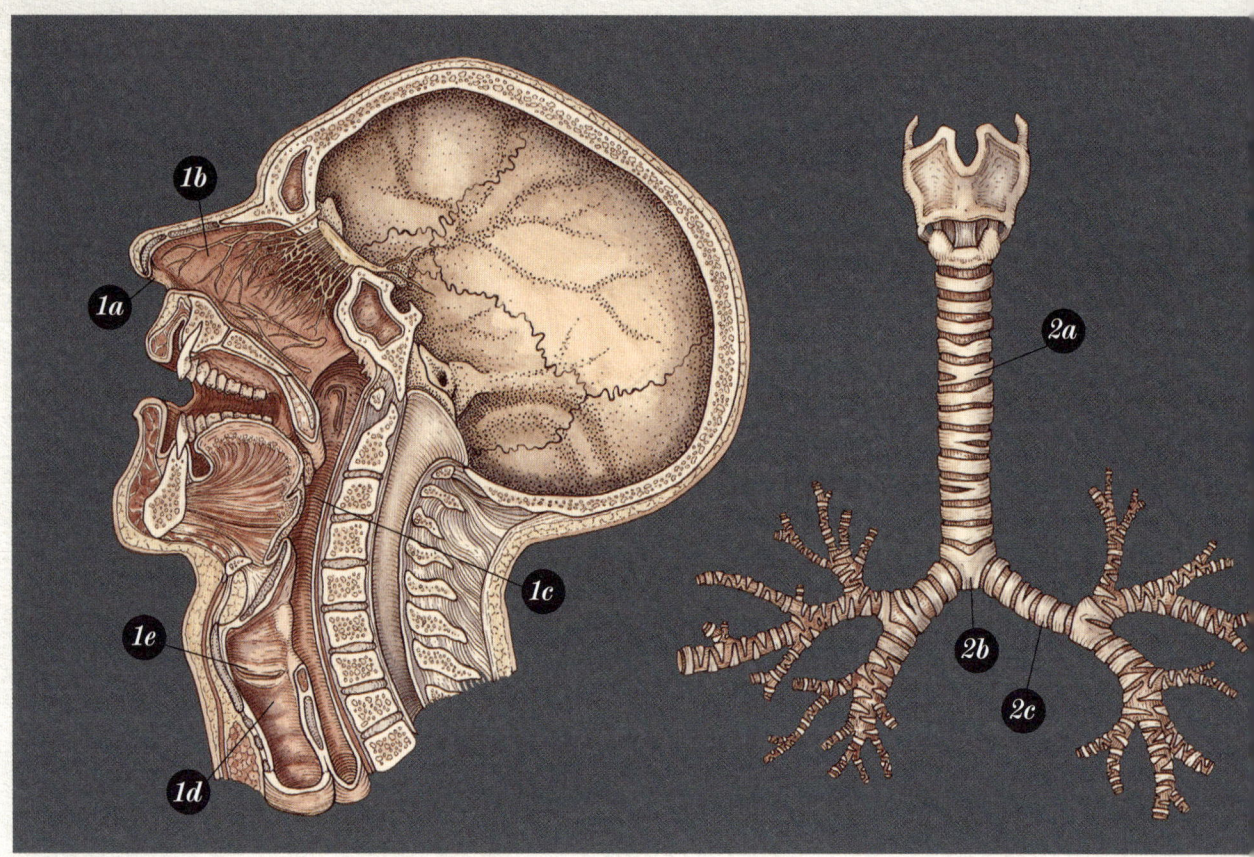

CIRCULATORY & RESPIRATORY SYSTEMS

The Respiratory Tract & Lungs

We breathe over 10,000 litres of air each day to keep our cells alive and healthy. Processing all this air is the job of the lungs, but first, air has to find its way into the body. For this, we need the respiratory tract.

Air is breathed in through the nostrils, where nasal hairs filter out dirt and dust particles. Then it enters the nasal cavity behind the nose where sticky mucus traps any remaining dust. From there, air travels through the pharynx (throat) to the larynx (voice box) where sound is made using two small flaps called vocal cords. Finally, air enters the trachea (windpipe), the pathway to the

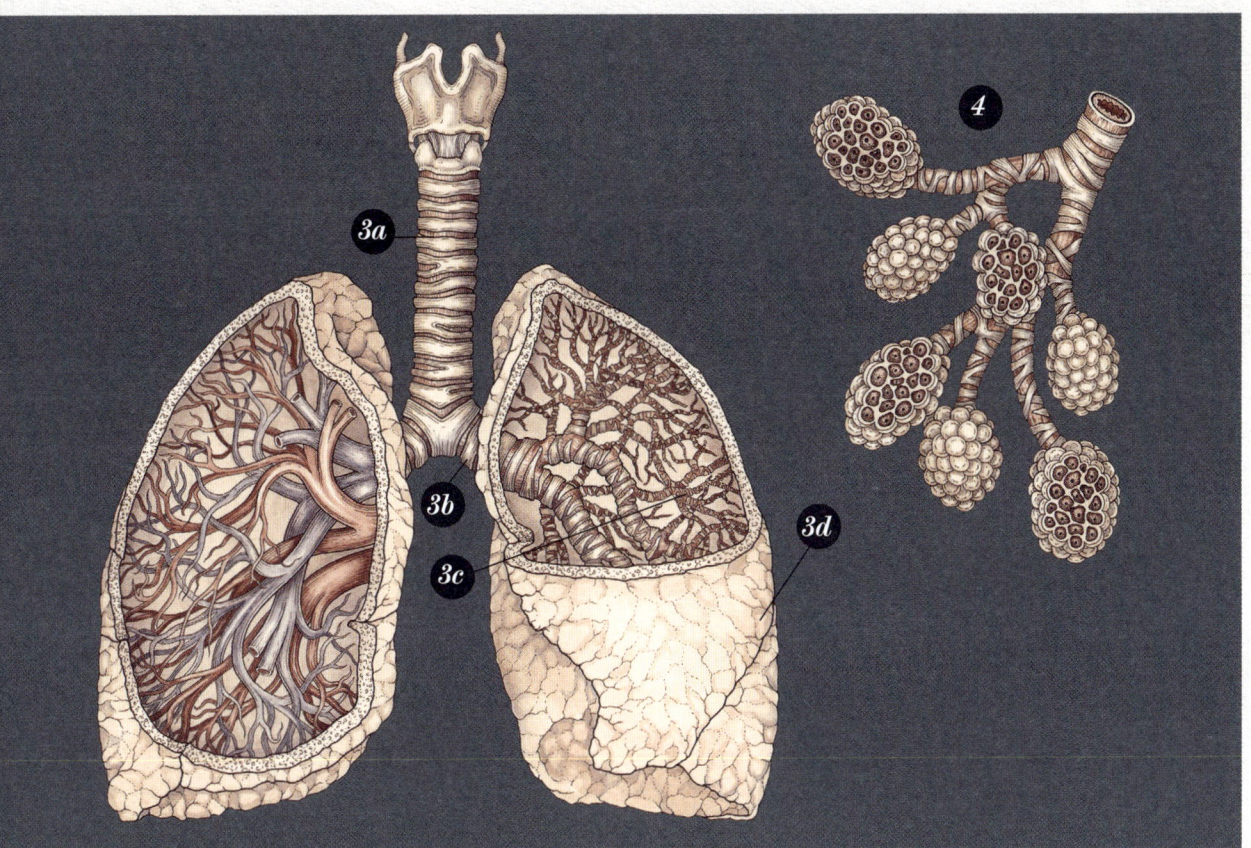

lungs. At its base, the trachea branches out into bronchi, two smaller pathways that send air into the lungs.

The lungs transfer oxygen from air into the bloodstream, and pass carbon dioxide from the bloodstream into the air to be exhaled. For this to happen, air travels through a network of tubes until it reaches sacs called alveoli. Each individual alveolus is covered in a tiny blood vessel called a capillary (see page 30), where oxygen and carbon dioxide are carried to and from the blood.

Key to plate

1. **Upper respiratory tract**
a) Nostrils
b) Nasal cavity
c) Pharynx (throat)
d) Larynx (voice box)
e) Vocal cords

2. **Lower respiratory tract**
a) Trachea (windpipe)
b) Carina: The branching point of the trachea into the two primary bronchi.
c) Bronchus

3. **Lungs**
a) Trachea
b) Bronchus
c) Bronchioles
d) Pleural membranes: Two thin, fluid-filled membranes that encase the lungs, allowing them to inflate and deflate.

4. **Alveoli (cross-section)**
The millions of alveoli in each lung group together to form small bunches.

> CIRCULATORY &
> RESPIRATORY SYSTEMS

Immune & Lymphatic Systems

The immune system is a collection of organs, tissues and cells that defend the body from harmful things. A key feature is the leukocyte (white blood cell), which attacks viruses and bacteria. It is found in the blood and in immune organs like the thymus, spleen, tonsils and lymph nodes. The largest of these organs is the spleen, which filters blood and makes leukocytes.

The lymphatic system is a large network of tubes, known as lymphatic vessels, and the lymph nodes. These are clumps of immune tissue in the neck, armpits and groin that act like sieves to filter out harmful things. The lymphatic vessels also mop up lymph, a watery substance that is squeezed out of the body's cells. Too much lymph would make parts of the body swell up, so the lymphatic vessels suck up any excess, clean it and empty it into large veins near the heart to be mixed with blood and pumped round the body.

Key to plate

1: **Tonsils**
Three sets of tonsils in the neck area help to fight infection.

2: **Lymph nodes in armpit**
These nodes are small collections of lymphoid tissue in the armpits, neck and groin region.

3: **Thymus gland**
The thymus gland sits in between the breastbone and the lungs. It is where special defence cells called T-lymphocytes mature.

4: **Thoracic duct**
This is the largest of the lymphatic vessels in the body. It transports lymph from the rest of the body to the veins near the heart, where the lymph returns to the blood as it circulates.

5: **Spleen**
A soft, dark-red organ shaped like a jellyfish. The spleen stores blood, filters it and makes white blood cells.

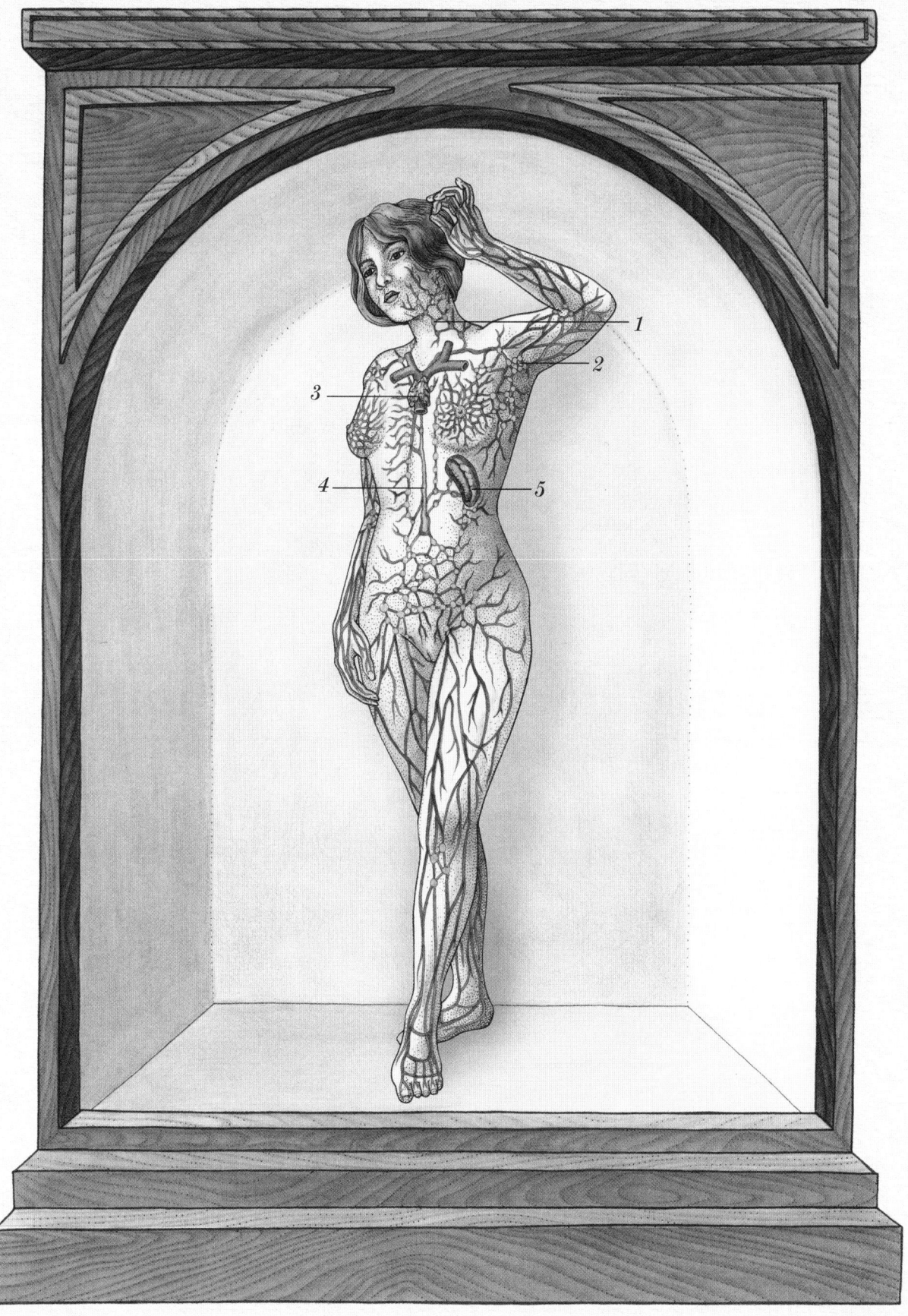

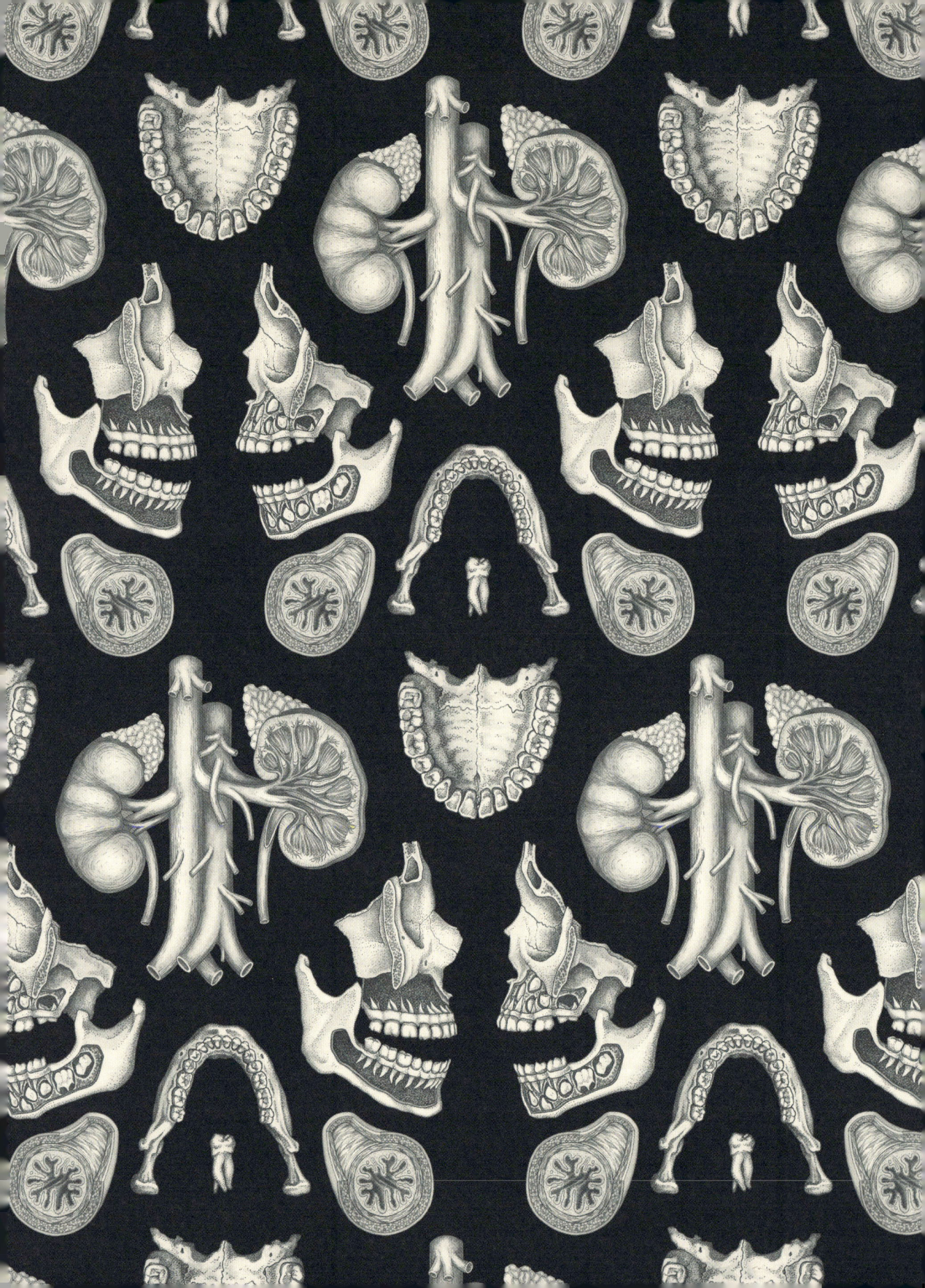

ANATOMICUM

Gallery 3

The Digestive & Urinary Systems

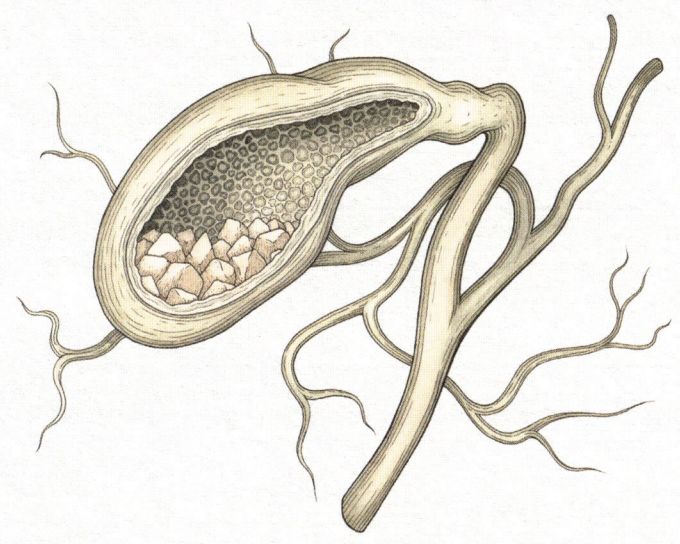

*The Digestive System;
Teeth; The Stomach;
The Intestines; The Liver;
The Pancreas & Gall Bladder;
The Urinary System & Kidneys*

THE DIGESTIVE &
URINARY SYSTEMS

The Digestive System

The digestive system is a clever food-processing plant, working all the time to take in food, break it down into the nutrients we need, and get rid of the waste that's left. Seven connecting organs – the mouth, pharynx (throat), oesophagus (food pipe), stomach, intestines, rectum and anus – form a direct path, called the digestive tract.

The process of breaking down food to make energy is called digestion. First, food is digested mechanically: broken down into smaller chunks by chewing food in the mouth, and then by mixing it up using muscles in the stomach. Then, food is digested chemically: special molecules called enzymes break nutrients like fats, proteins and carbohydrates into even smaller parts.

The liver, gallbladder and pancreas all help the digestive tract by releasing different chemicals into it. This combination of nerve signals (see page 54) and hormones (see page 48) communicate with the brain to control the processes of eating, digestion and excretion. Emotions can affect the digestive system, too – that's why you sometimes feel sick when you're excited or nervous.

Key to plate

1: **Mouth**

2: **Throat (pharynx)**

3: **Oesophagus (food pipe)**
A long, muscular tube that connects the pharynx to the stomach.

4: **Stomach**

5: **Small intestine**
A long passageway that joins the stomach to the large intestine. Digested food passes through the small intestine, where the nutrients it contains are absorbed into the body's bloodstream.

6: **Large intestine**
The waste products of digested food pass through the large intestine. Any remaining water is absorbed back into the bloodstream. The remaining dry waste, called faeces (poo) travels to the rectum and anus, where it willl exit the body.

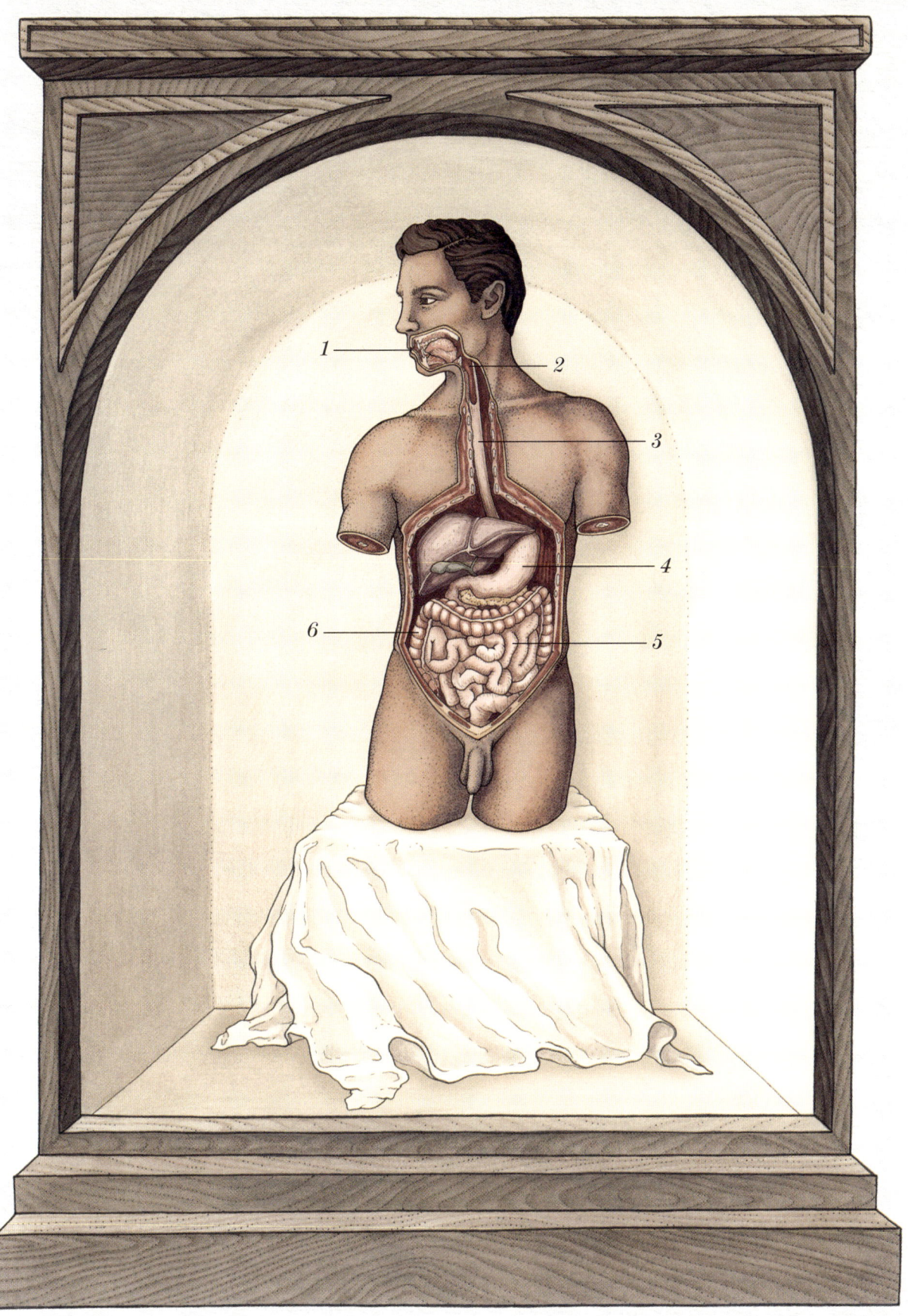

THE DIGESTIVE &
URINARY SYSTEMS

Teeth

The job of the teeth is to make sure food is soft and smooth, so it can then be swallowed. Babies are born without any teeth at all, but children have a full set of 20 'milk teeth' by the time they are three. As they grow up, these baby teeth are slowly pushed out by 32 adult teeth, including four wisdom teeth at the very back of the mouth. This final set of adult teeth cannot repair themselves and need to last an entire lifetime. Decay (rot) can cause holes to appear, and these need to be fixed by a dentist.

There are several types of teeth, each with a different job to do. Incisors are sharp, thin teeth at the front of the mouth, used to slice into food. Next to them are the pointed canines, used to bite, tear or hold food. Premolars and molars, at the back of the mouth, are flat and squarish with ridges on the top, designed to crush and grind food while you chew.

Each tooth has several layers. The outer layer of enamel protects the crown (top) of the tooth and is full of vitamins like calcium, which gives teeth their white colour. Underneath is a hard substance called dentine, which protects the dental pulp, a soft cushioning around the sensitive blood vessels and nerves. At the bottom of the tooth is the root, which is buried in the gums. Individual teeth are held firmly in place in the jaw by fibrous joints (see page 16), covered in a tough substance called cementum.

Key to plate

1: Adult skull
The roots of the teeth reach deep into the jawbones.

2: Child's skull
Here we can see the permanent teeth developing behind the milk teeth. During childhood, they eventually push out the milk teeth.

3: Types of adult teeth
a) Molars (12)
b) Premolars (8)
c) Canines (4)
d) Incisors (8)

4: Upper jaw (maxilla), from below

5: Lower jaw (mandible), from above

6: Structure of a tooth
a) Enamel
b) Dentine
c) Pulp
d) Root
e) Cementum

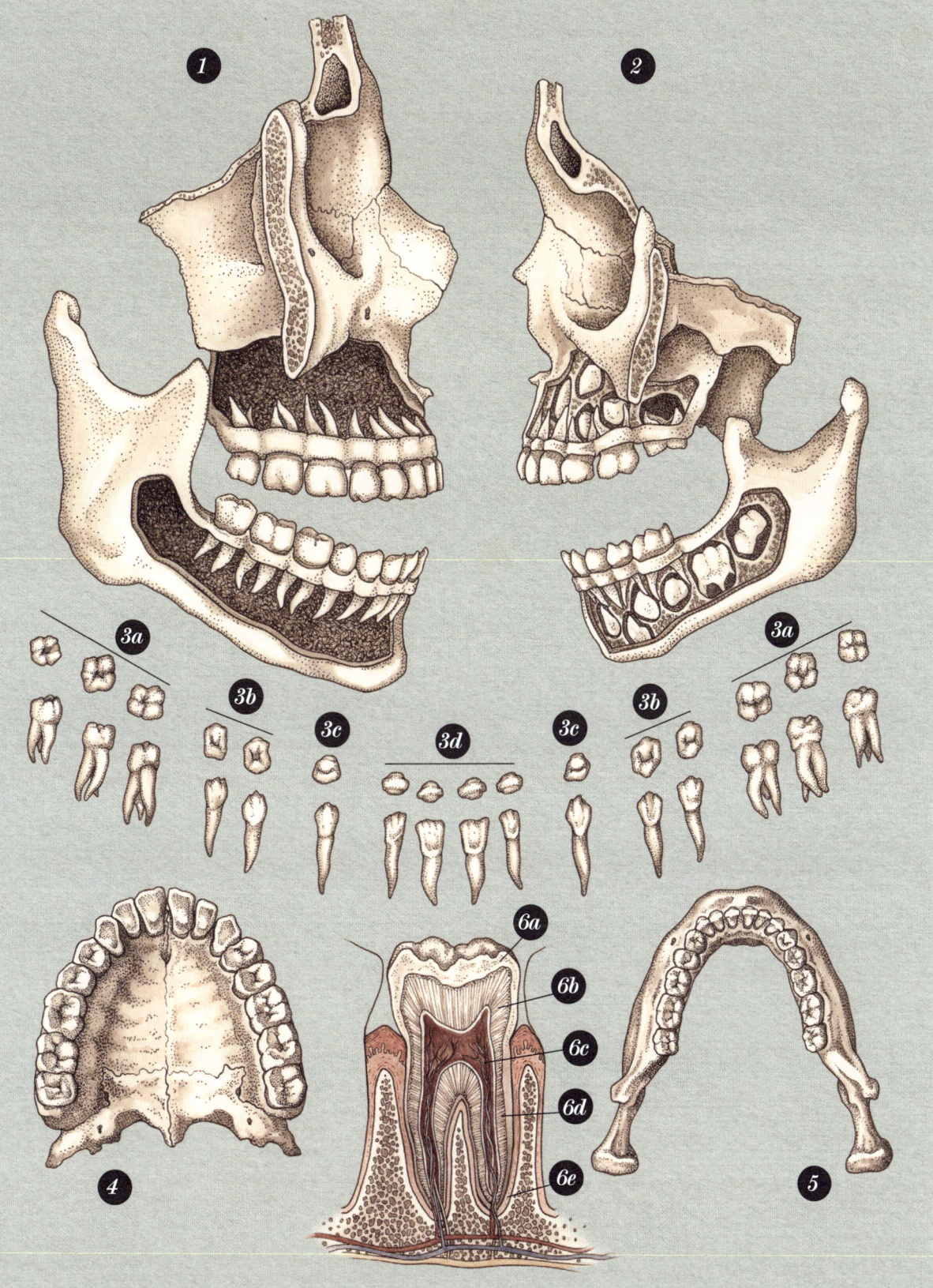

> THE DIGESTIVE & URINARY SYSTEMS

The Stomach

After food has been swallowed, it is sent to the stomach. The stomach stores the food we eat and 'churns' it to mix with stomach acid. The resulting mixture, a fluid called chyme, is passed on to the next part of the digestive tract.

Cells in the stomach lining produce 1.5 litres of gastric juice (stomach acid) every day. It chemically digests food by breaking down long molecules into smaller ones, and also helps to kill any dangerous bacteria. A layer of mucus on the stomach lining stops the stomach wall being damaged by the acidic juice.

Have you ever heard your stomach 'rumble' when you're hungry? This is just the sound of the stomach as it churns. When the stomach is empty, it fills with gas, and without any food to muffle the noise the growling sounds are louder. At its fullest, an adult stomach can hold one to two litres of food and drink. The inside walls of the stomach are folded into ridges that can fan out to expand, stretching the walls as the stomach fills up. Special sensors can tell if the stomach is stretched or not, giving you a feeling of 'fullness' or hunger.

Food can stay in the stomach for as little as 20 minutes or for hours, depending on what has been eaten. Cooked fruit and vegetables are easy to digest, but rich, greasy food can take several hours. Once chyme (digested food) is ready to leave the stomach, a special valve at the stomach's base will let small amounts through to the small intestine.

Key to plate

1: **Oesophagus (food pipe)**

2: **Cardiac sphincter**
This ring of smooth muscle acts like a valve to let food into the stomach. It also prevents food and stomach acid from travelling back up into the oesophagus.

3: **Layers of the stomach wall**
a) Oblique muscles
b) Circular muscles
c) Longitudinal muscles

4: **Stomach**
Thick folds, called rugae, stretch as the stomach fills and allows the stomach to expand.

5: **Pyloric sphincter**
A ring of smooth muscle which controls the release of chyme from the stomach to the small intestine.

6: **Duodenum**
This is the first part of the small intestine.

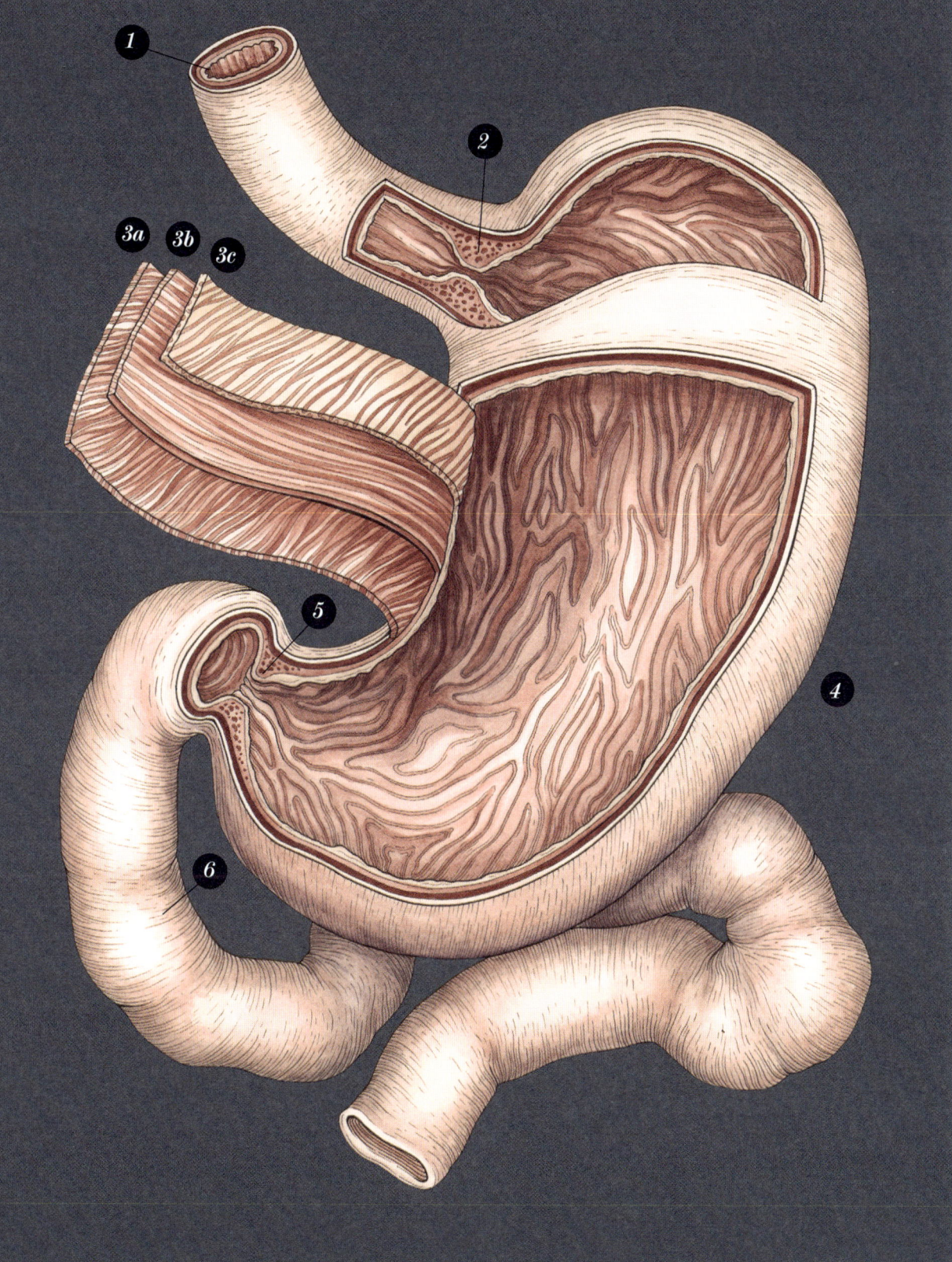

The Intestines

The long tubes of the small and large intestines are where the main process of digestion takes place. The small intestine is actually the longest part of the digestive system; the terms 'small' and 'large' refer to the width of the intestines, rather than their length. There are three parts to the small intestine: the duodenum, the jejunum and the ileum. The duodenum is where acidic chyme from the stomach meets alkaline fluids from other organs, reducing its acidity. After this, chyme is propelled along the jejunum and ileum by muscle contractions, being digested and absorbed as it goes.

The walls of the small intestine are very long, tightly folded and covered with millions of tiny finger-like structures called villi. This increases its surface area; stretched out, it would cover an area of about 250 square metres. Its huge size lets nutrients and water be absorbed quickly and easily, passing straight into the blood vessels within the villi.

Once chyme reaches the colon (large intestine), the body has absorbed most of the nutrients it needs. A mixture of water and waste materials is left behind. As the chyme travels through the colon, its water content is absorbed back into the body. The remaining solid waste, called faeces (poo), is stored in the rectum before exiting the body through the anus.

--- *Key to plate* ---

1: **Small intestine**
The long tube where most nutrients are absorbed during digestion.

2: **Colon (large intestine)**
This is where water is absorbed from food waste before it leaves the body.
a) Rectum
b) Anus

3: **Cross-section of small intestine**
a) Inner mucosa: This layer has a folded surface lined with villi, so it has a high surface area for absorbing nutrients.
b) Submucosa: This layer carries blood vessels, nerves and lymphatic vessels.
c) Muscular layers: Two connecting layers of muscle contract to propel food along the digestive tract.
d) Outer covering (serosa): A connective tissue coating.

4: **Villi of the small intestine**
Fingerlike projections called villi line the small intestine.

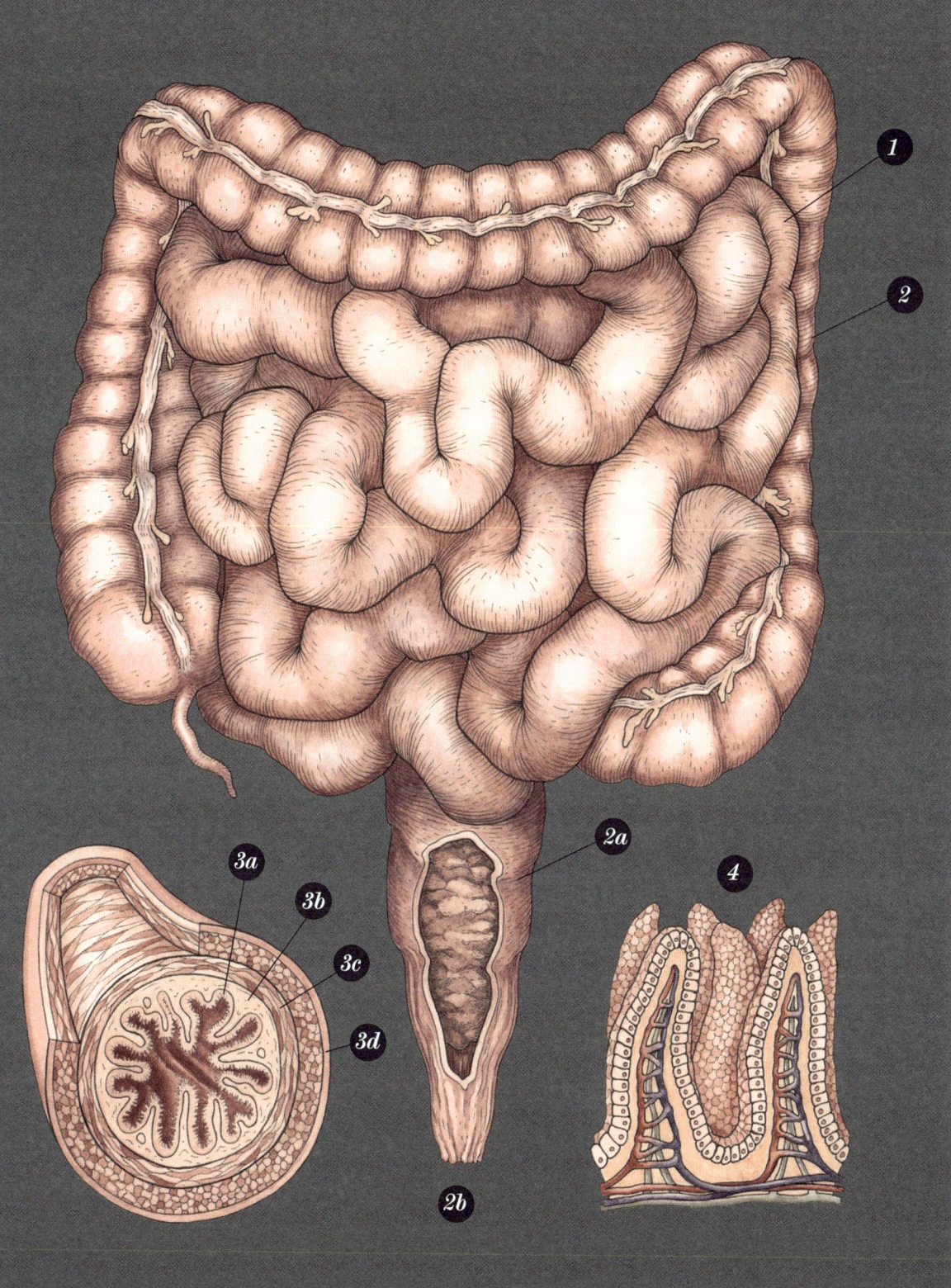

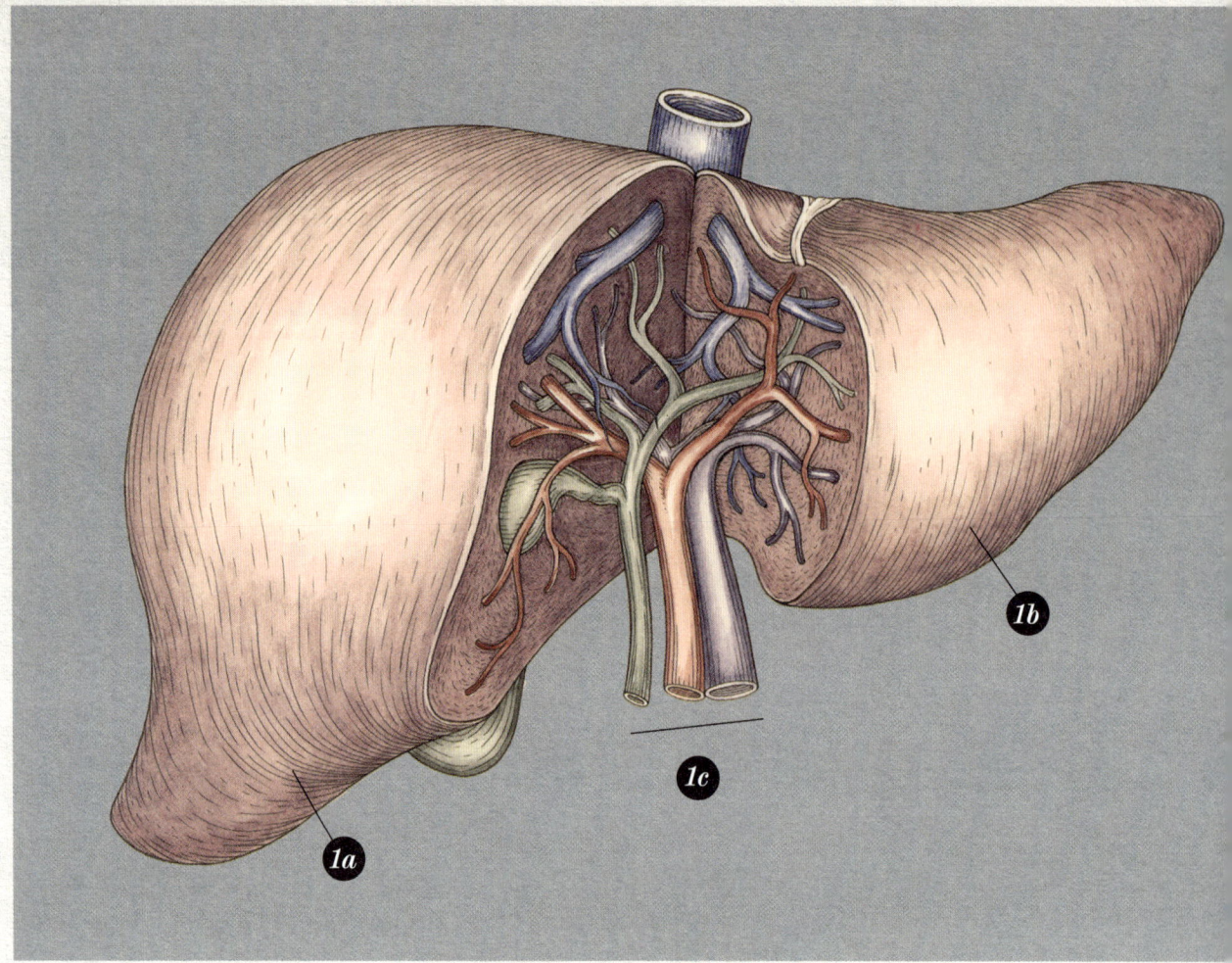

THE DIGESTIVE & URINARY SYSTEMS

The Liver

The liver, the largest organ in the body, keeps the blood in the body healthy. It is roughly triangular with four different lobes, or parts, and its deep-red colour comes from its large blood supply. It serves three major roles: cleaning the blood, making bile and storing energy.

First, the liver cleans the blood by removing anything harmful. Often it can change toxins (harmful substances) into molecules that are safe for the body, but if it can't, it sends the toxins to the digestive system to exit the body as faeces, or to the kidney to leave the body as urine. Secondly, the liver makes bile, a thick, yellow-green liquid that helps the body digest fat. Bile is either sent to the small intestine straight away, or sent to the gallbladder (see page 48) to

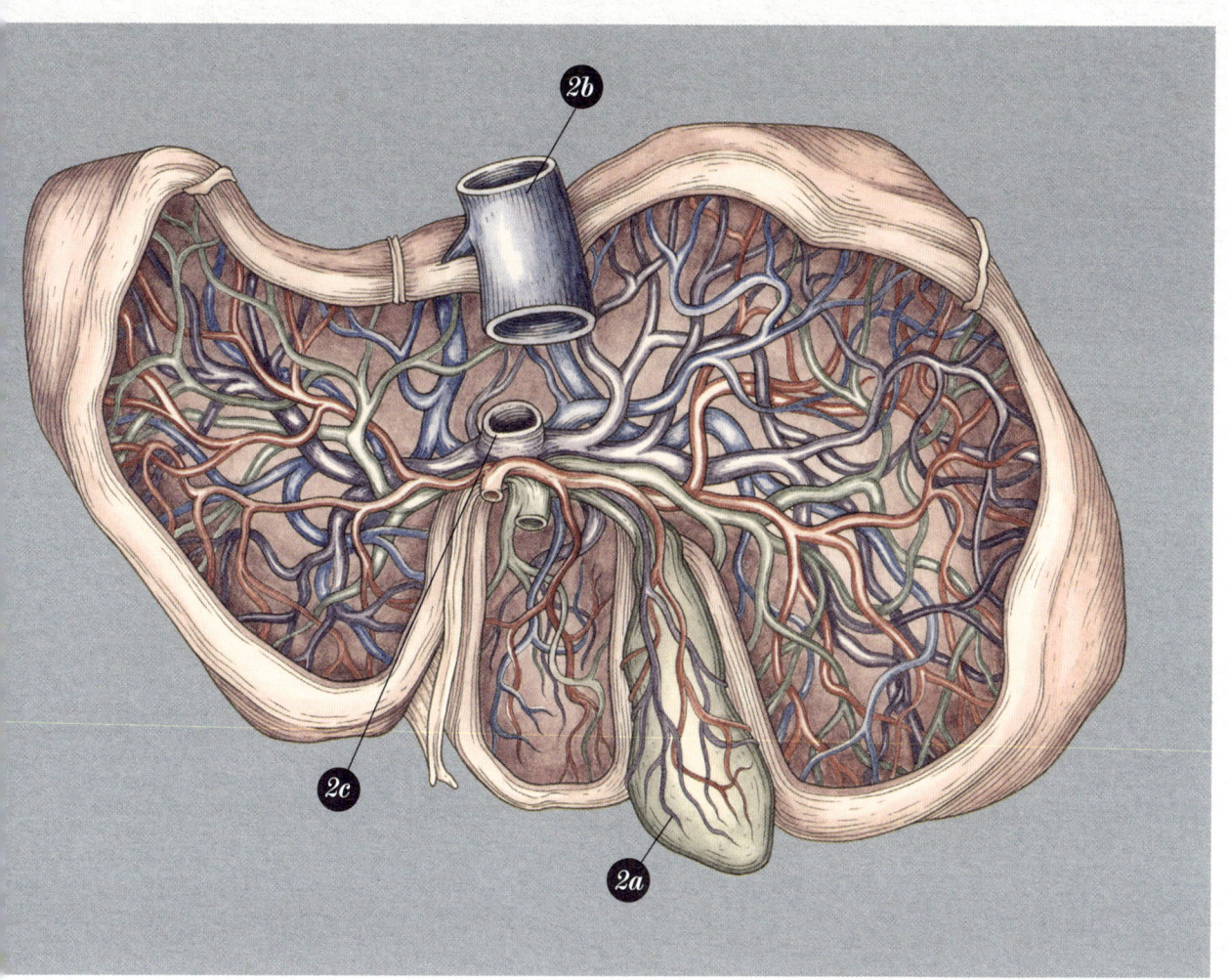

be stored. Thirdly, the liver stores and produces energy, like a battery. The liver is 'charged' by blood coming from the small and large intestines, packed full of nutrients that are absorbed during digestion.

The liver has an amazing feature that no other organ in the human body has: it can regenerate. Damage to the liver by disease or toxins can stop it working properly and make people very ill, but if the damaged parts are removed, the rest of the liver can actually grow back.

Key to plate

1: **Liver, front view**
a) Right lobe
b) Left lobe
c) Hepatic portal system: This is where nutrient-rich blood arrives at the liver from the small and large intestines.

2: **Liver, inside and back view**
a) Gallbladder
b) Inferior vena cava: Blood leaving the liver exits here on its way back to the heart.
c) Hepatic portal vein

The Pancreas & Gallbladder

The pancreas has an important role to play both in the digestive system and the endocrine system (see page 70). It sits near the stomach with its head in the curve of the duodenum, the first part of the small intestine. This position allows it to release a fluid called pancreatic juice directly into the intestines. This neutralises acidic chyme before it goes any further into the digestive system.

The pancreas is a glandular organ, which means it produces and releases chemicals. When a gland releases a substance straight into an organ or tissue, like the pancreas does, it is called an exocrine function. The pancreas also releases chemicals directly into the blood, a process called an endocrine function. Two of these chemicals are hormones called insulin and glucagon, which control sugar levels. If sugar levels are too low, the pancreas produces glucagon to tell the liver to release sugar. If sugar levels are too high, the pancreas produces insulin to reduce the amount of sugar in the blood.

Bile is another liquid crucial for digestion. It is made in the liver but is stored in a small muscular bag called the gallbladder. The gallbladder shares the entrance to the small intestine with the pancreas.

Key to plate

1: **Gallbladder**
A pouch-shaped organ that stores the bile made by the liver. Bile helps to digest fats, and is released into the duodenum of the small intestine after eating.

2: **Duodenum**
The first part of the small intestine, containing the openings of the common bile duct and the pancreas.

3: **Pancreas**
Pancreatic juice is produced in the pancreas and emptied into the duodenum.

4: **Gallbladder with gallstones**
The salts within bile can form little deposits, called gallstones, that sit in the gallbladder. If one escapes, it can block the tube between the gallbladder and the duodenum and cause severe pain.

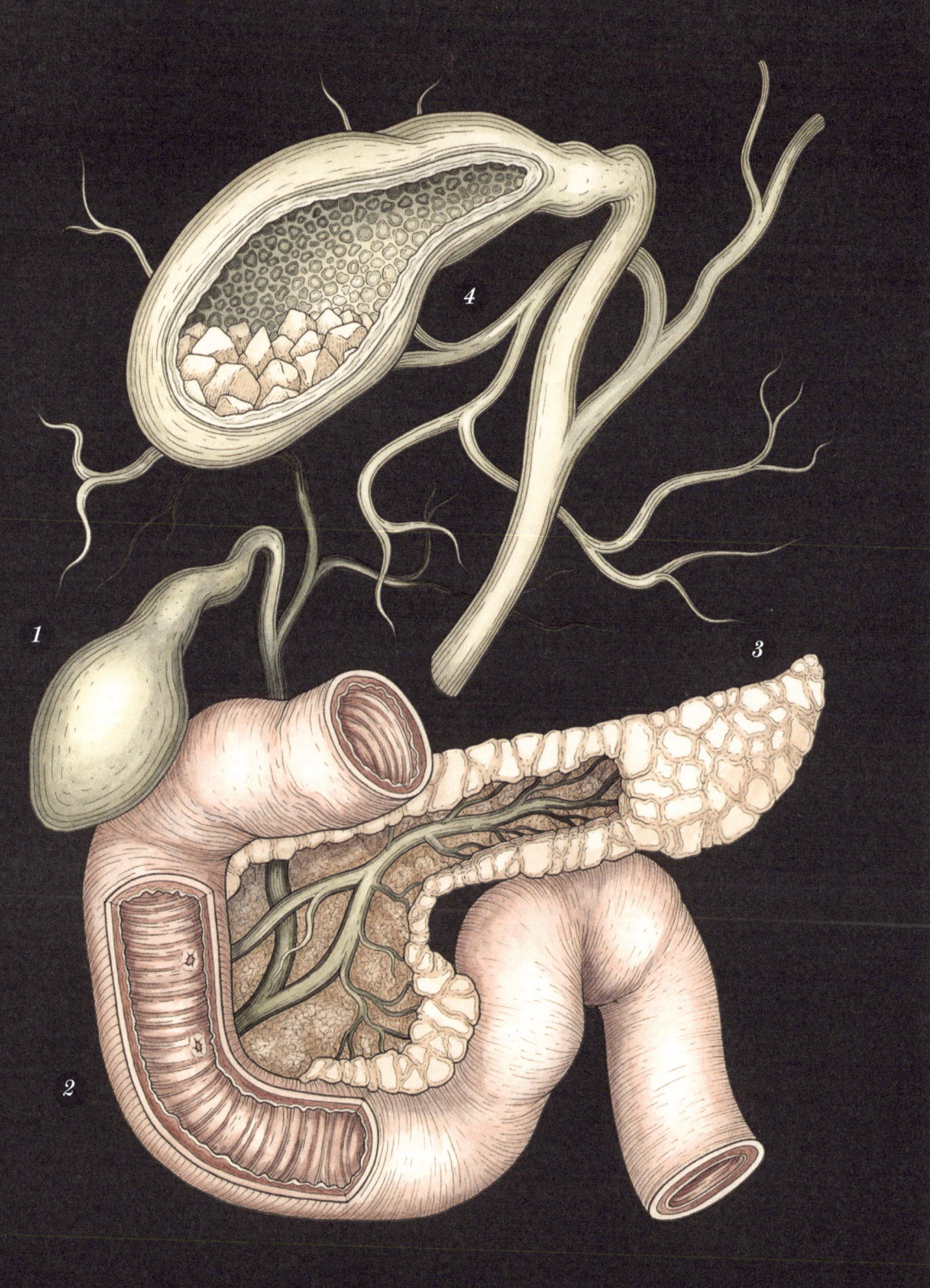

The Urinary System & Kidneys

The urinary system is the body's plumbing system, a collection of organs that take waste products from the blood and turn them into urine (pee). The kidneys do most of the work, since this is where urine is made. Passages and storage areas make up the rest of the system.

The two kidneys are working all the time to clean the body's blood. They do this by pumping blood through tiny filters called nephrons. These remove any waste products made during the body's chemical reactions, pass toxins into our urine, and re-absorb anything the body needs to keep. The kidneys also control the balance of water and salts in the body.

Once urine has been made in the kidneys, it drips down two thin tubes called ureters, each about 30 centimetres long. Smooth muscles contract and push the urine down to be stored in the muscular bag called the bladder.

The bladder stretches as it fills with urine and can hold about 500 to 600 millilitres. Once it's full, special nerve sensors in the bladder wall let the brain know that you need to urinate. This is when urine leaves the body through a thin pipe called the urethra.

Key to plate

1: **Blood supply to the kidney (renal artery)**
Oxygenated blood from the heart enters the kidneys here.

2: **Blood supply from the kidney (renal vein)**
Deoxygenated blood leaves the kidneys here.

3: **Kidneys**
The right kidney is slightly lower, because the liver takes up a lot of room.

4: **Ureters (right and left)**
The ureters are two long muscular tubes. They connect each kidney to the bladder, providing a pathway for urine.

5: **Bladder**
The bladder sits in the pelvis and stores urine.

6: **Sphincter**
The sphincter is a ring of muscle controlling the emptying of the bladder.

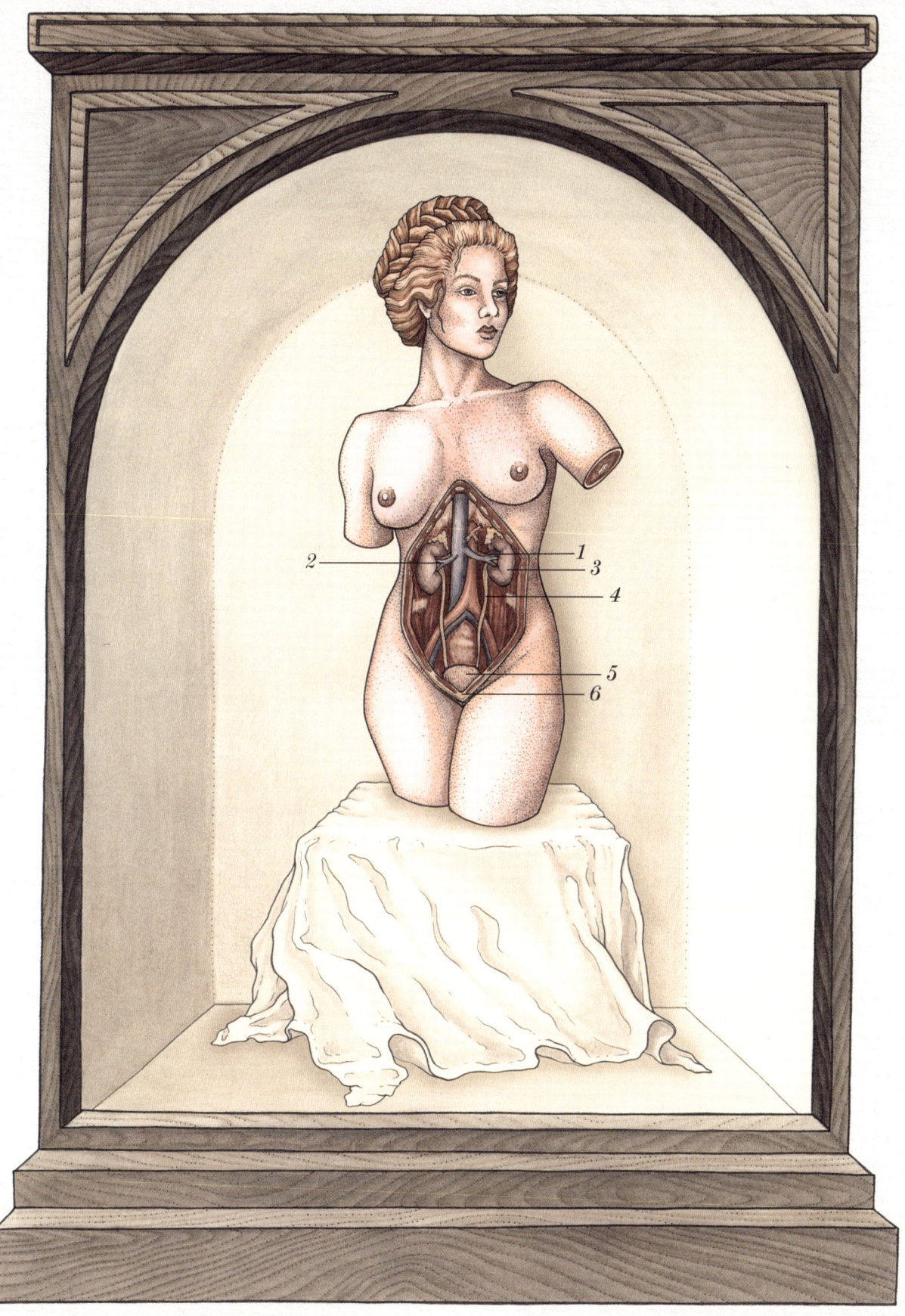

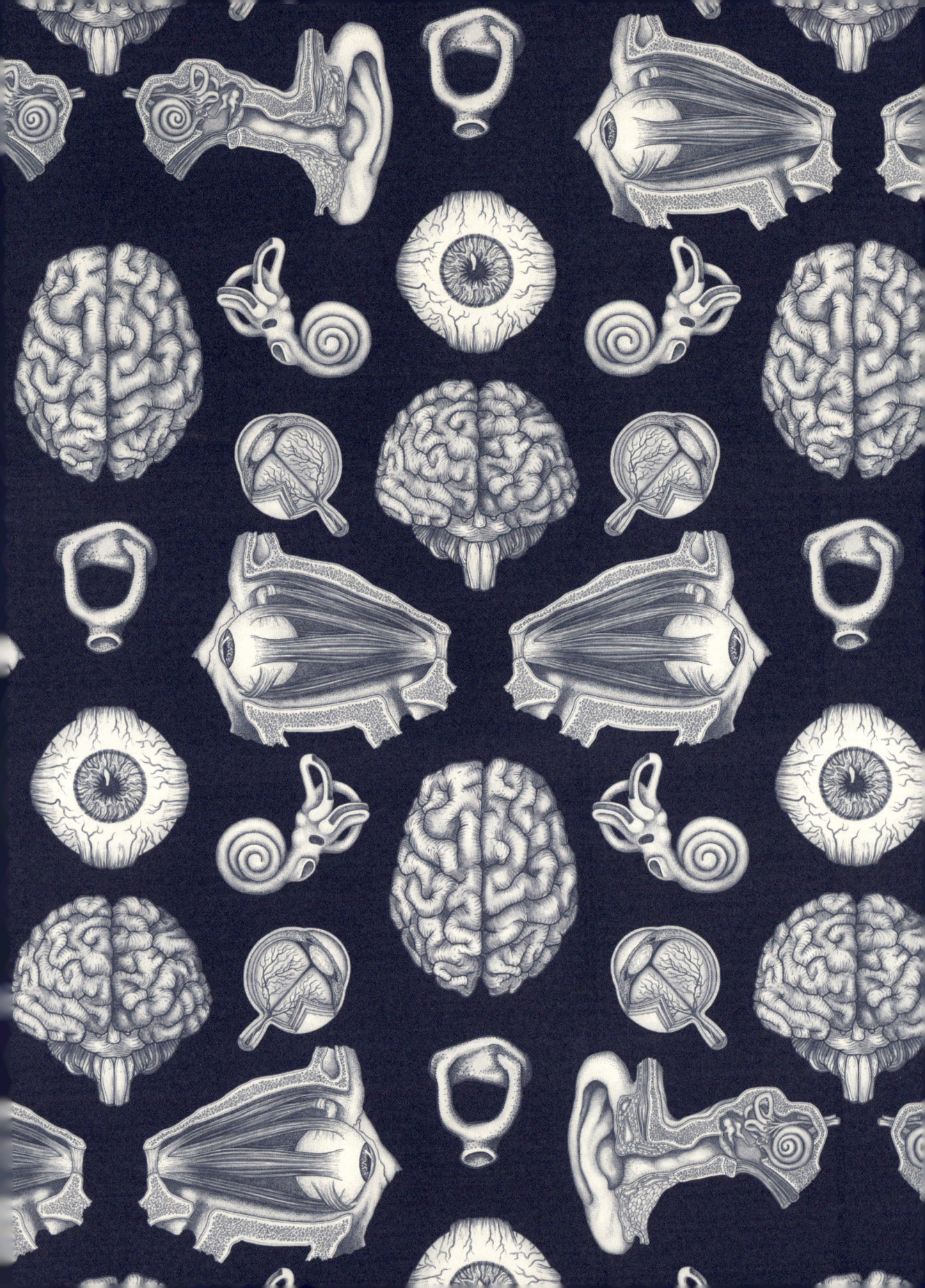

ANATOMICUM

Gallery 4

The Nervous System & Special Senses

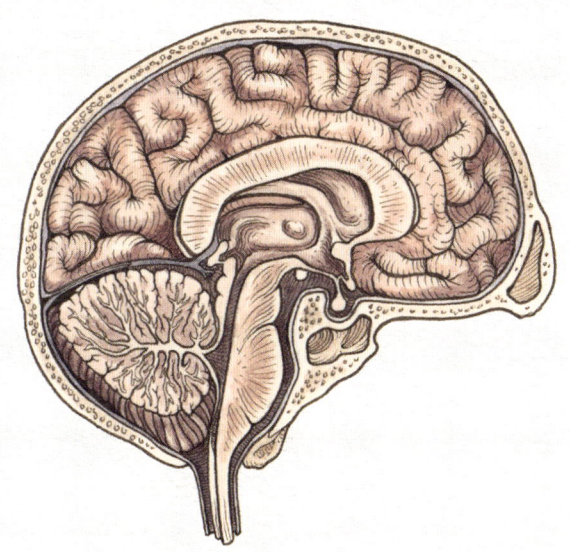

The Nervous System;
The Central Nervous System;
The Peripheral Nervous System;
The Eyes; The Ears;
The Nose & Tongue; Skin

The Nervous System

Sometimes described as the most amazing supercomputer ever known, the brain processes hundreds of thousands of messages a second. These messages bring you information from the outside world and from inside your body, and travel to and from the brain as electrical signals. They travel along pathways called nerves, passing each other like traffic on a busy two-way street.

Once the brain has taken in information, it can send a message back to the body in response. For instance, if a car appears as you're crossing the road, your eyes will see the car and send a message to the brain. The brain will process the car as possibly dangerous, and send signals to make you step back on to the pavement. Even more impressive is the fact that this exchange takes less than a second to happen. Electrical signals travel along nerves at speeds of over 100 metres per second.

At the hub of the nervous system are the brain and spinal cord. They make up the central nervous system (CNS), and control most of the body's actions. These vital organs sit well-protected within the skull and vertebrae of the spine. The spinal cord then connects to the peripheral nervous system (PNS), which extends out into the rest of the body and is responsible for collecting sensory messages (from the sense organs), and delivering motor signals (orders to move) between the CNS and other body parts.

--- *Key to plate* ---

1: **Central nervous system (CNS)**
a) Brain: This is the control centre for the entire nervous system. All conscious (voluntary) and unconscious (involuntary) actions go through the brain.
b) Spinal cord: This long bundle of nerves connects the brain to the peripheral nervous system.

2: **Peripheral nervous system (PNS)**
a) Spinal nerves: The spinal cord branches out to the left and right sides in 31 matching pairs of spinal nerves. Each pair supplies a specific part of the body.
b) Peripheral nerves: These run between body organs and the limbs to send messages to and from the brain and spinal cord.

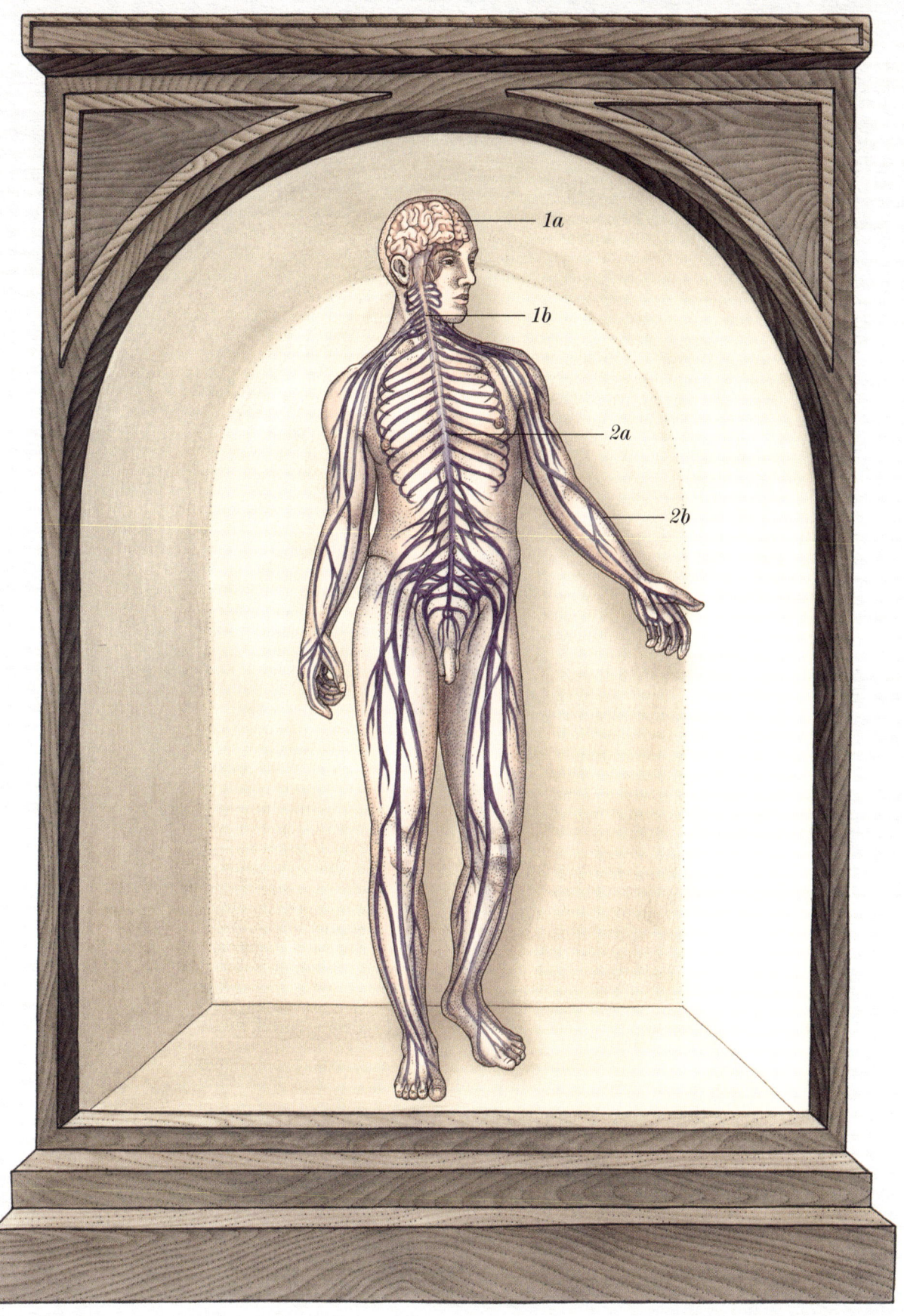

THE NERVOUS SYSTEM
& SPECIAL SENSES

The Central Nervous System

The human brain makes up only three per cent of our overall body weight, but it uses about 20 per cent of the body's energy – much more than any other organ. This is because the brain controls everything we do, from movement and breathing to thoughts, emotions and memories.

The outside of the brain, the cortex, looks wrinkled because of its many folds of brain tissue. Thanks to these folds, its billions of nerve cells can fit within the small space of the skull.

The largest part of the brain is the cerebrum, which controls our intelligence, conscious movements (the actions we do on purpose) and sensations (feelings). It is split into two halves linked by a 'bridge' of tissue. The right side of the brain controls the left side of the body, and the left side of the brain controls the right side of the body. Areas within each half control different things. For example, the frontal lobe is important for making decisions, planning, thinking and our emotions, which all help to shape our personalities.

At the very back of the brain is the cerebellum, a small structure that looks like a walnut and helps us control our movements and balance. Hanging from the middle of the brain is the brainstem, which connects the brain to the spinal cord and controls basic activities needed to stay alive, such as breathing.

Key to plate

1: **Brain and spinal cord**
The spinal cord extends from the centre of the brain, connecting it to the peripheral nervous system.

2: **Brain, front view**
There are two halves of the brain (known as the cerebral hemispheres). The folds, or gyri, of the brain increase its surface area and make it look wrinkled.

3: **Brain, cross-section**
a) Cerebrum
b) Cerebellum
c) Brainstem
d) Spinal cord

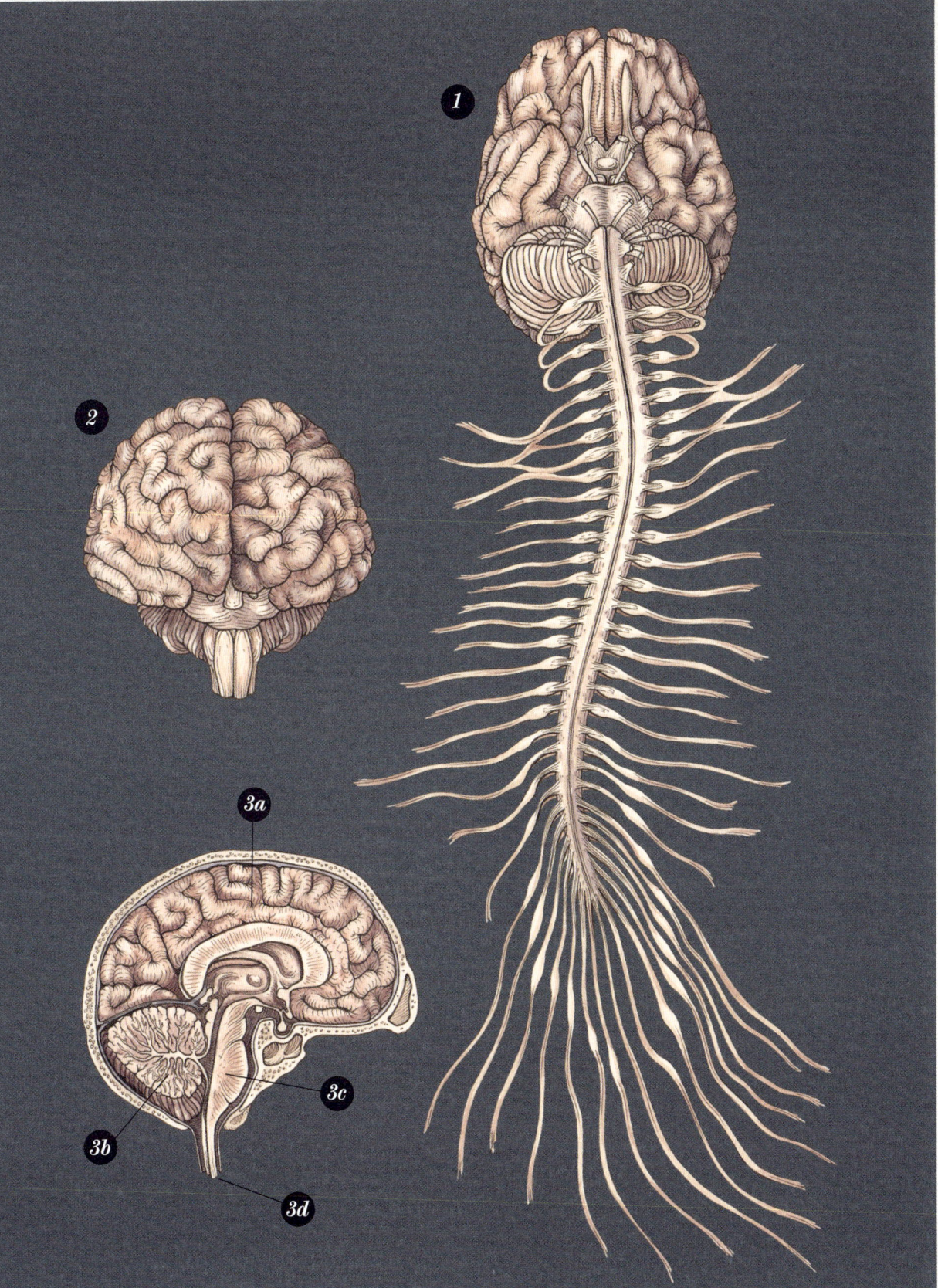

THE NERVOUS SYSTEM
& SPECIAL SENSES

The Peripheral Nervous System

Individual nerves are made of bundles of neurons (thin nerve cells), which run through the body like electrical wires. Most neurons have one main fibre (a long threadlike structure running through them) called an axon, which sends out electrical signals. Axons have an insulating layer, called a myelin sheath, to protect them.

Within the neuron, smaller fibres called dendrites collect incoming electrical signals from other neurons. In between neurons are gaps called synapses. Electrical signals can't jump across these gaps, so axons release chemical signals to leap across them. The dendrites 'catch' the signal and pass it on via their own axon. All this happens at an incredible speed.

The human body contains around 95 to 100 billion neurons. Most of these are in the brain and spinal cord, but the rest are in the peripheral nervous system (PNS). This is a network of nerves that begins at the spinal cord and branches out into 31 pairs of spinal nerves, communicating between the central nervous system (CNS) and the body's muscles and sense organs.

―――――――――――――― *Key to plate* ――――――――――――――

1: Reflex arc
If your hand comes near a candle, pain sensors in the hand send a message to the spinal cord. The spinal cord processes the danger and sends motor signals telling the hand to move away from the flame. Reflex reactions like this allow the body to react at the first sign of danger.

2: Anatomy of a spinal nerve
a) Axon: The central part of a nerve along which electrical signals are sent.
b) Myelin sheath: This fatty layer acts as an insulating coating for the axon.
c) Fascicle: This is the name for a bundle of axons. .
d) Perineurium: This is a coating around fascicles.
e) Blood vessels

3: Close up of a neuron (nerve cell)
a) Cell body
b) Dendrite
c) Axon
d) Myelin sheath
e) Nerve ending

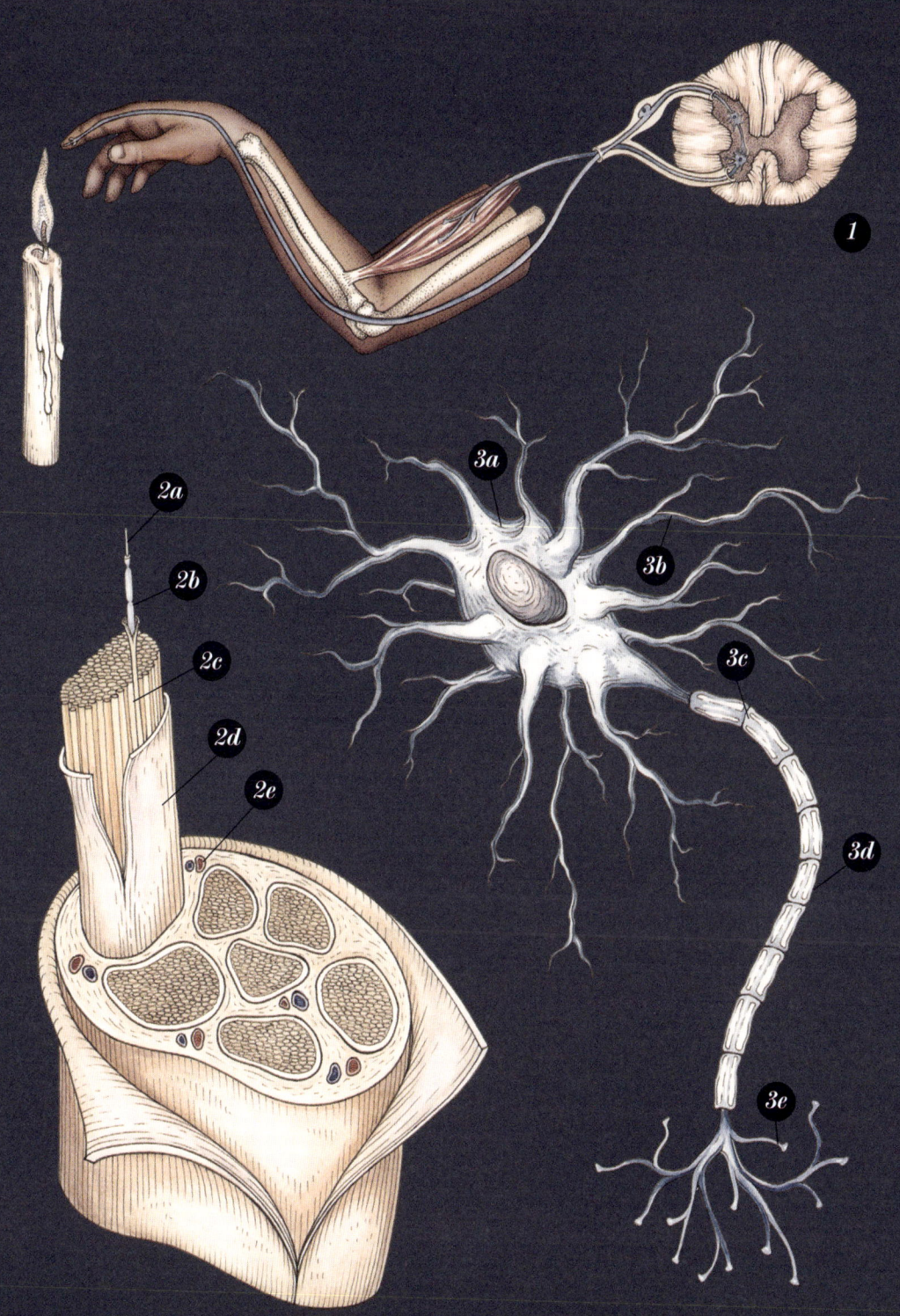

> THE NERVOUS SYSTEM
> & SPECIAL SENSES

The Eyes

The eyes are a pair of ball-shaped organs, set within the skull in two spherical holes called orbits. Their job is to receive light and turn this information into electrical signals that the brain can understand as images.

Light enters the eye through a small hole called the pupil and is focused by the cornea, a clear shield that also protects the eye. Around the pupil is the iris, a ring of coloured muscle that gives eyes their colour and adjusts the size of the pupil. In bright light, the iris makes the pupil smaller, reducing the amount of light that can pass through. In low light, the pupil expands to let more light in. After light has entered the eyes it passes through the lens, which bends the light and focuses it onto the back of the eyeball.

The back of the eye is called the retina. It has millions of light-detecting sensor cells which translate light messages into electrical signals for the brain. These electrical signals are sent to the brain via an optic nerve at the back of each eye. The whole process happens in a fraction of a second.

--- *Key to plate* ---

1: **Retina (back of the eye)**
The sensory layer at the back of the eyeball containing the optic nerve, which links the eye to the brain.

2: **Eye muscles**
a) Front view
b) Side view
Three pairs of skeletal muscles attach to the outside of each eye, letting them move, roll and even cross.

3: **Iris and pupil**
The pupil is a hole in the centre of the iris, a ring of pigmented tissue. The pupil is where light enters the eye to travel towards the retina.

4: **Inside the eyeball**
a) Cornea
b) Iris
c) Pupil
d) Lens
e) Vitreous humour: A clear, gel-like liquid filling the eyeball
f) Retina
g) Optic nerve: This carries sensory information from the eye to the brain.

5: **Tear production**
a) Tear (lachrymal) gland
b) Tear duct
Eyelashes, eyelids and tear production all protect the eyes from damage.

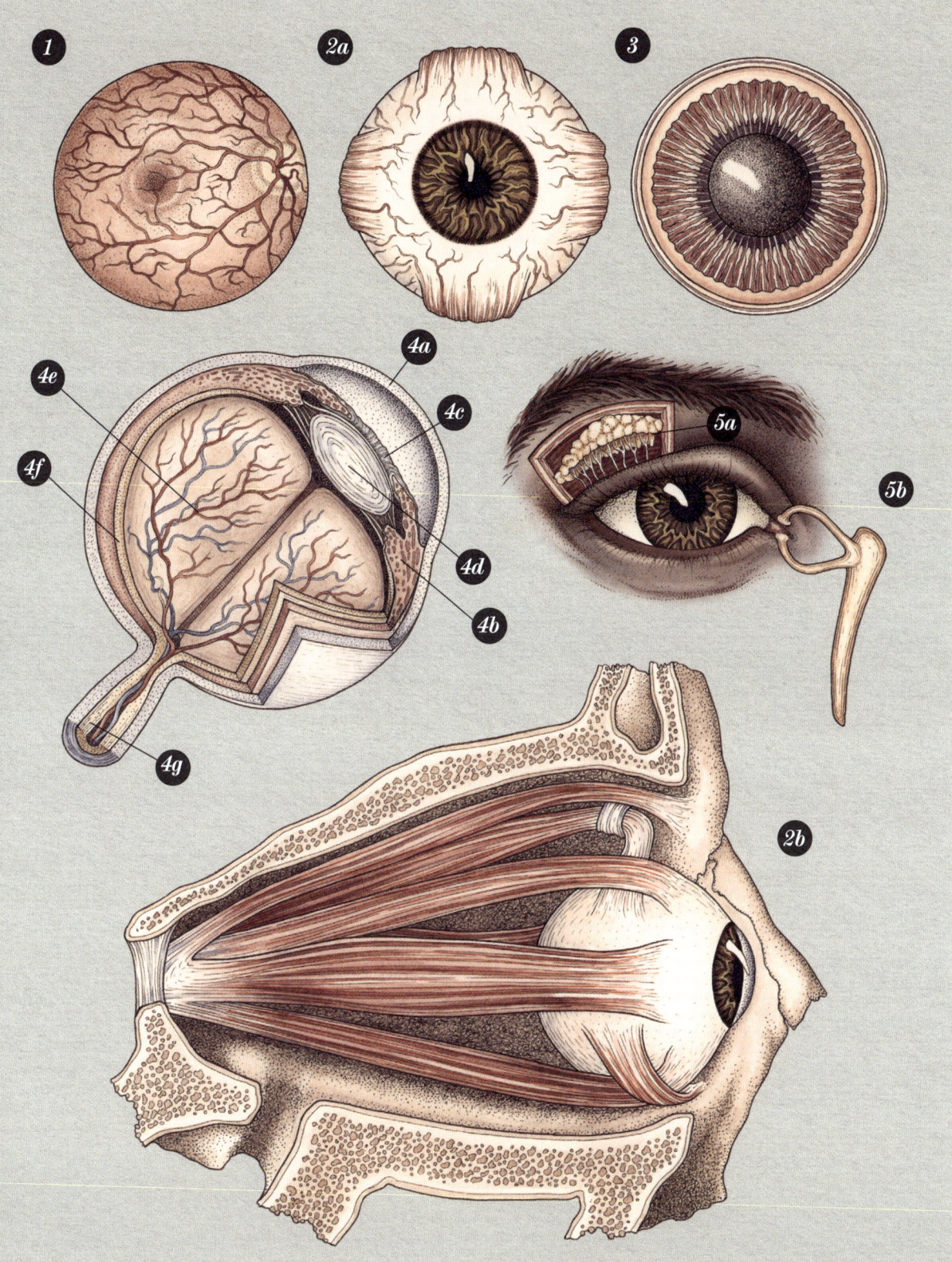

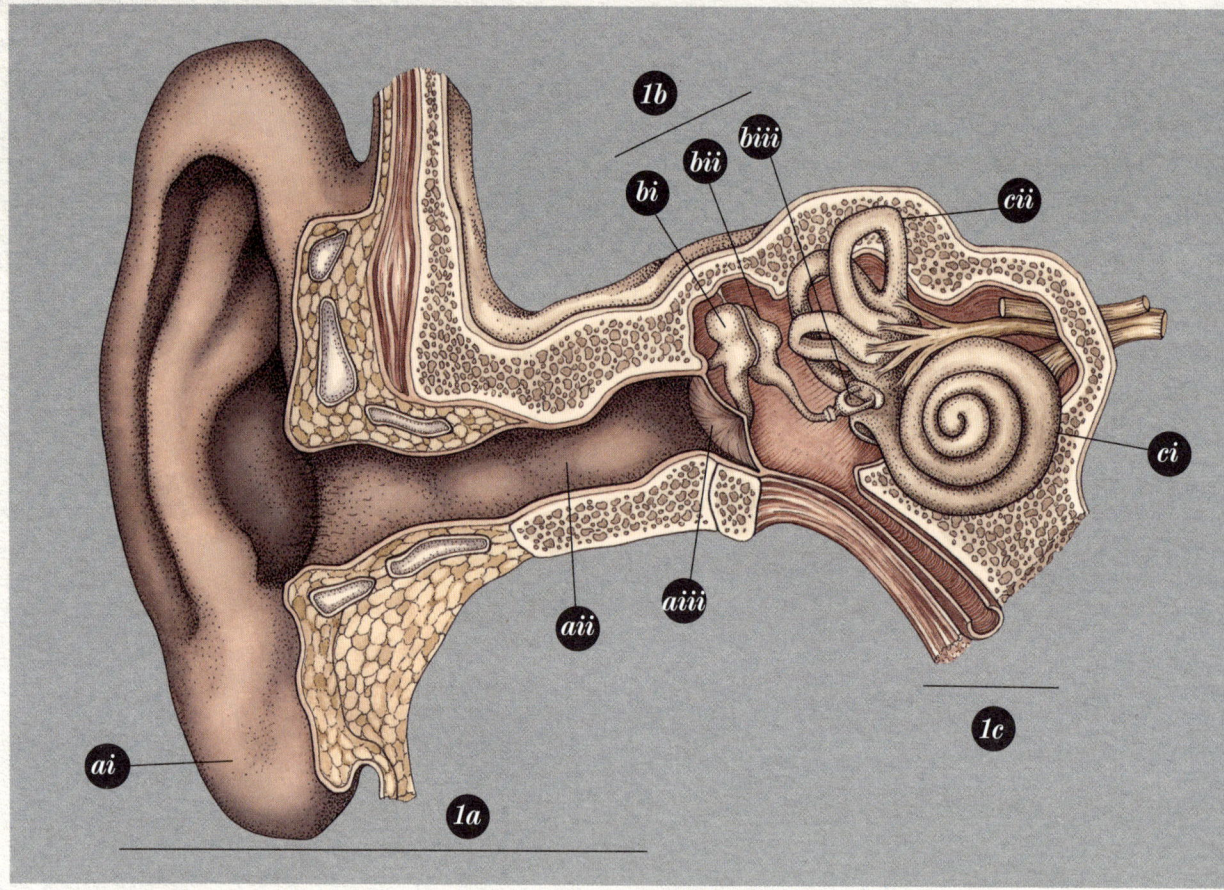

THE NERVOUS SYSTEM & SPECIAL SENSES

The Ears

The ear is actually split into three areas: the outer ear, which funnels sound; the middle ear, which turns sound into vibrations; and the inner ear, which turns vibrations into nerve signals for the brain to use. The outer ear collects sounds from all around us and sends them into the ear canal, a small passageway leading to the eardrum. The eardrum vibrates when sound waves reach it. On the other side of the eardrum is the middle ear, an air-filled space with three tiny bones known as the ossicles. These bones, called the hammer, anvil and stirrup, connect the eardrum to a part of the inner ear called the cochlea. The cochlea is filled with fluid and tiny hairs. When sound waves are funnelled by the outer ear into the eardrum and vibrate, the movement passes through the ossicles to the cochlea. The fluid and hairs move, making electrical signals that are sent to the brain to be decoded as sounds.

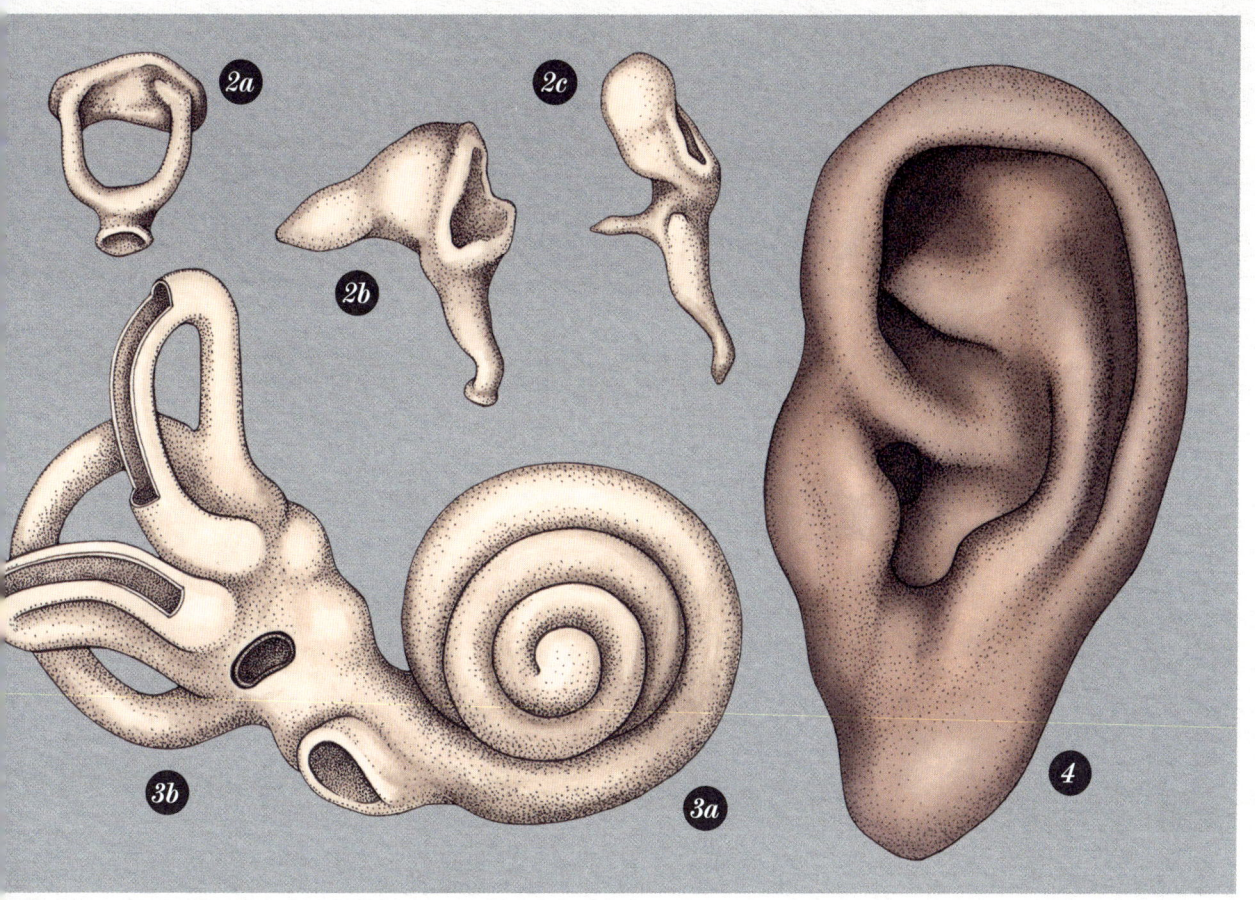

Ears also affect our sense of balance. Within the inner ear are thin rounded tubes called semicircular canals, filled with fluid and tiny hairs like the cochlea. The fluid and hairs move every time we change the position of the head, telling the brain which way up we are.

--- *Key to plate* ---

1: **Ear**
a) Outer ear: The pinna *(i)* leads to the ear canal *(ii)* and the ear drum *(iii)*.
b) Middle ear: The hammer *(i)*, anvil *(ii)* and stirrup *(iii)* send the vibrations of the ear drum to the inner ear.
c) Inner ear: The cochlea *(i)* and semicircular canals *(ii)* convert sound wave vibrations into electrical signals for the brain.

2: **Ossicles**
a) Stapes (stirrup)
b) Incus (anvil)
c) Malleus (hammer)

3: **Inner ear**
a) Cochlea
b) Semicircular canals

4: **Pinna (outer ear)**
The outer ear acts as a funnel for sounds to enter the middle ear.

The Nose & Tongue

For modern humans, smell and taste aren't usually considered essential, although they might bring back distant memories or alert us to rotten food. But many years ago, our senses were much more important for our survival. The reaction to bad smells or tastes helped to keep the body safe from life-threatening infections found in dirty water or bacteria-filled food.

Smell works by detecting odour molecules floating in the air around us. When we breathe, they enter the nostrils and pass into the nasal cavity, a large space behind the nose. The roof of the nasal cavity contains millions of receptor cells that find odours and turn the 'smell' into an electrical impulse. This signal travels to the brain via a connection called the olfactory nerve.

Our sense of smell and taste are closely linked. Food tastes different if our ability to smell is taken away, like when you have a heavy cold. Thousands of taste sensors (taste buds) on the top of the tongue detect chemicals in the food we eat and send messages to the brain. There are four basic flavours of food that we can detect: sweet, sour, salty and bitter. A fifth taste category has also been suggested, called umami, or 'savoury'.

Key to plate

1: Nose
a) External nose: Mostly made of cartilage, the external nose is where odour molecules will enter the nasal cavity through the nostrils *(i)*.
b) Nasal cavity: This space inside the skull contains sensors that link to the olfactory nerve *(i)*, which detects odour molecules and transmits the sensory impulse towards the brain.

2: Tongue
The tongue sits in the oral cavity and is made up of several muscles. Many thousands of taste buds cover the top surface and are responsible for detecting one of the five different categories of taste sensation: sweet, salty, sour, bitter and umami.

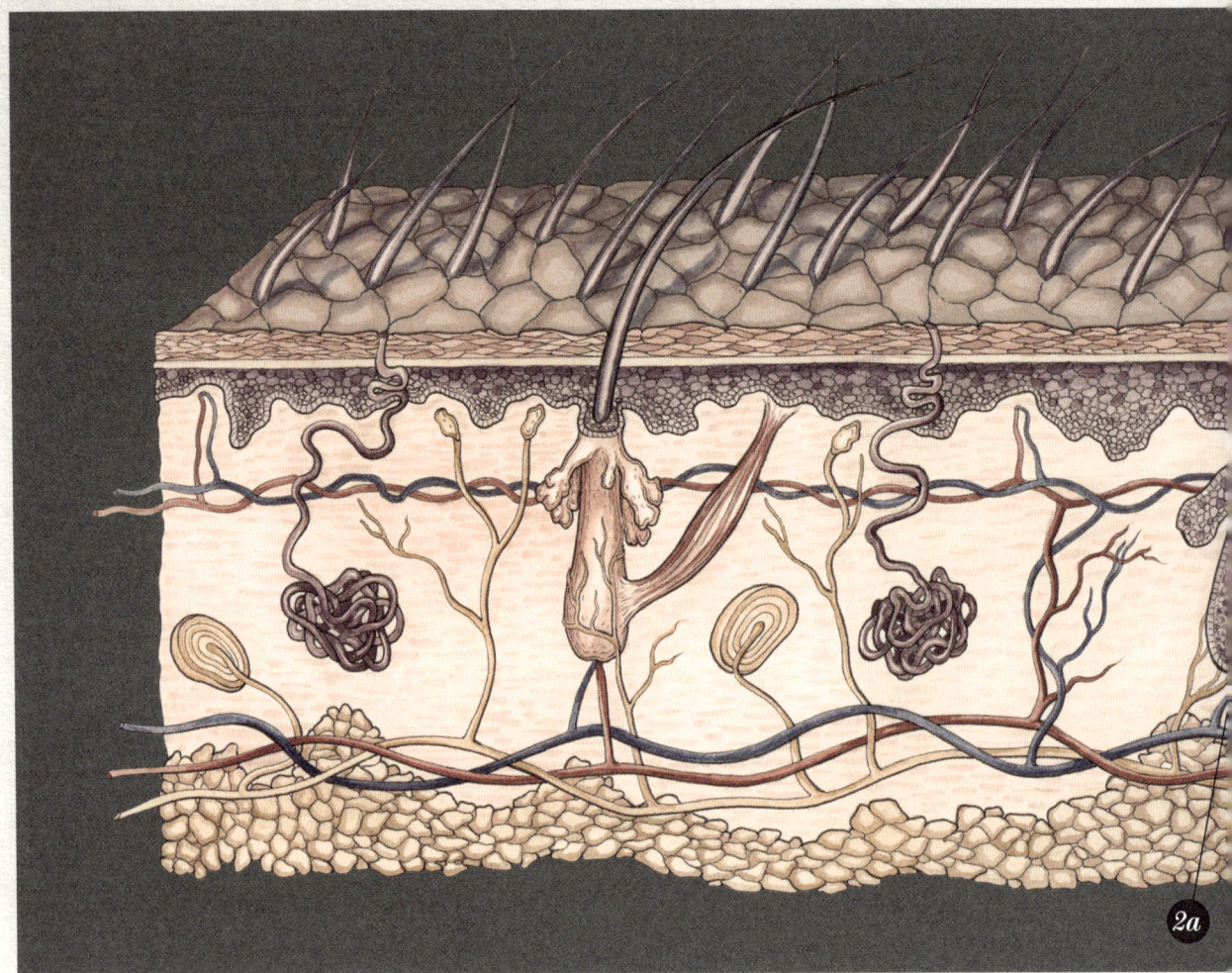

THE NERVOUS SYSTEM
& SPECIAL SENSES

Skin

Along with sight, sound, smell and taste, touch is an important sense, which lets us feel different sensations. Tiny touch sensors lie deep within the skin, which forms our whole outer body covering and creates a barrier between us and the outside world.

Skin is made up of two layers. The top layer, the epidermis, is a protective, waterproof wrapping around the body. Skin cells in the epidermis are always growing, multiplying and moving up to the surface of the skin as if they are on a conveyor belt. The very top cells are dead, and millions of skin cells fall off each day. Other cells in the epidermis produce melanin, a substance that shields the skin from sun rays. Underneath the epidermis is the dermis, a thicker layer

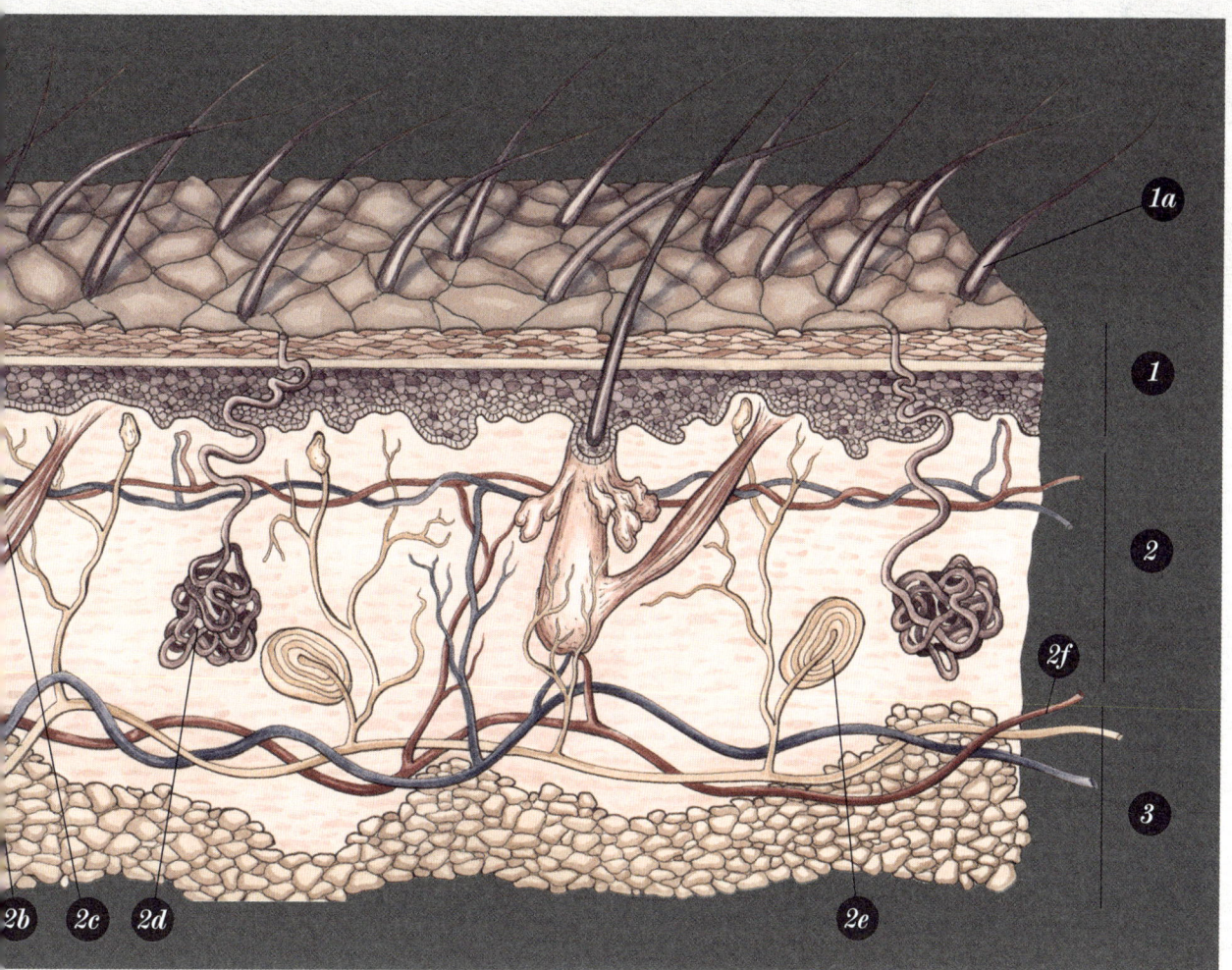

made from strong and stretchy proteins. It contains hair, sweat glands and millions of nerve endings – the sensory receptors that give us our sense of touch. A sense of touch is crucial for keeping us safe; without it we would not be able to feel our feet on the ground as we walk, to hold and control objects or to feel pain. Pain in particular is crucial to protecting us from harm, as it alerts the body to danger.

Key to plate

1: **Epidermis**
The top layer of skin, made from sheets of skin cells.
a) Hair shaft

2: **Dermis**
a) Hair root
b) Sebaceous gland
c) Arrector pili muscle: This pulls hairs upwards in 'goosebumps'.
d) Sweat gland
e) Sensory receptor
f) Dermal blood vessels

3: **Hypodermis**
The underlying fat layer.

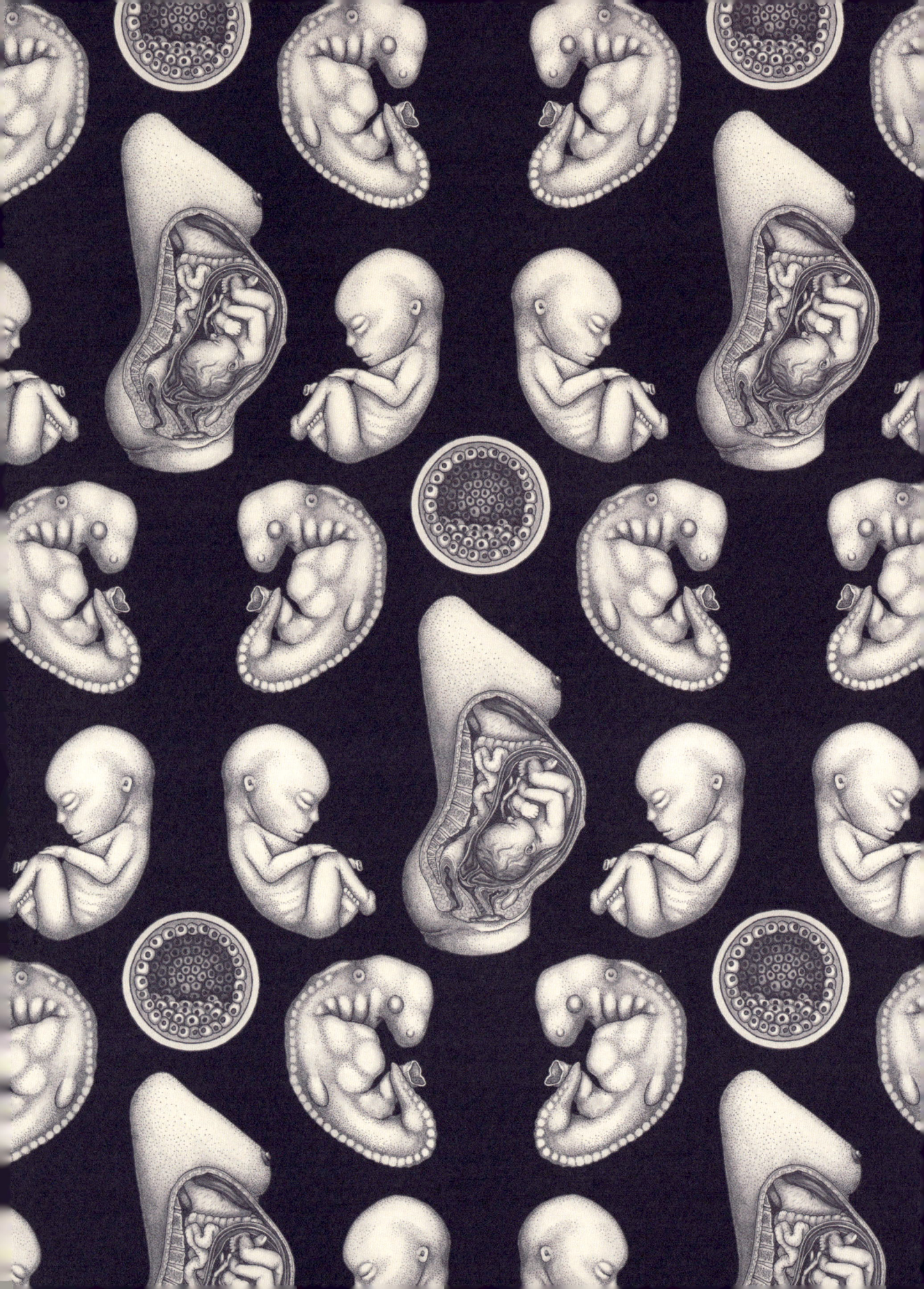

ANATOMICUM

Gallery 5

The Endocrine & Reproductive Systems

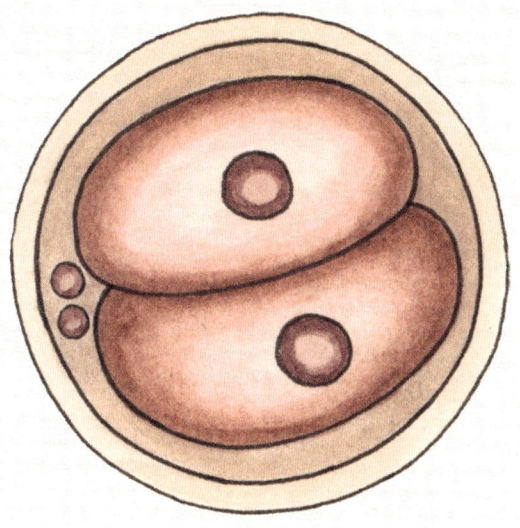

*Endocrine System; Puberty;
Male Reproductive System;
Female Reproductive System;
Development of a Baby*

> THE ENDOCRINE & REPRODUCTIVE SYSTEMS

Endocrine System

Chemical messengers called hormones circulate in the blood, delivering instructions to all parts of the body and controlling our growth, sleep and even our moods. Just like the nervous system, hormones let our body parts 'talk' to one another. The difference is that hormones travel in the blood, so their messages take longer to be delivered than nervous signals – a bit like the difference in time between sending an email and sending a letter.

Hormones are made by special cells in the glands and organs of the endocrine system. One of the main endocrine organs is the pancreas (see page 48). Another important part of the endocrine system is the adrenal glands, which are above the kidneys and produce the powerful hormone adrenaline. Adrenaline makes your heart beat faster, your breathing rate increase and your pupils get bigger. This happens automatically when adrenaline prepares your body for the 'fight-or-flight' response. This intense reaction is usually because of a physical threat, but it can have emotional triggers such as stress or anxiety, too.

Key to plate

1: **Hypothalamus**
This sends messages to the pituitary gland, telling it to produce hormones that affect emotions and control hunger, thirst and body temperature.

2: **Pineal gland**
This produces hormones that regulate sleep.

3: **Pituitary gland**
This secretes growth and development hormones.

4: **Thyroid gland**
This produces hormones that control metabolism.

5: **Thymus**
This produces hormones that help to keep T-cells (a type of lymphocyte) healthy.

6: **Adrenal glands**
These produce 'fight-or-flight' hormone adrenaline.

7: **Ovaries (female only)**
These produce and release female sex hormones.

8: **Testes (male only)**
These produce and release male growth and sex hormones like testosterone.

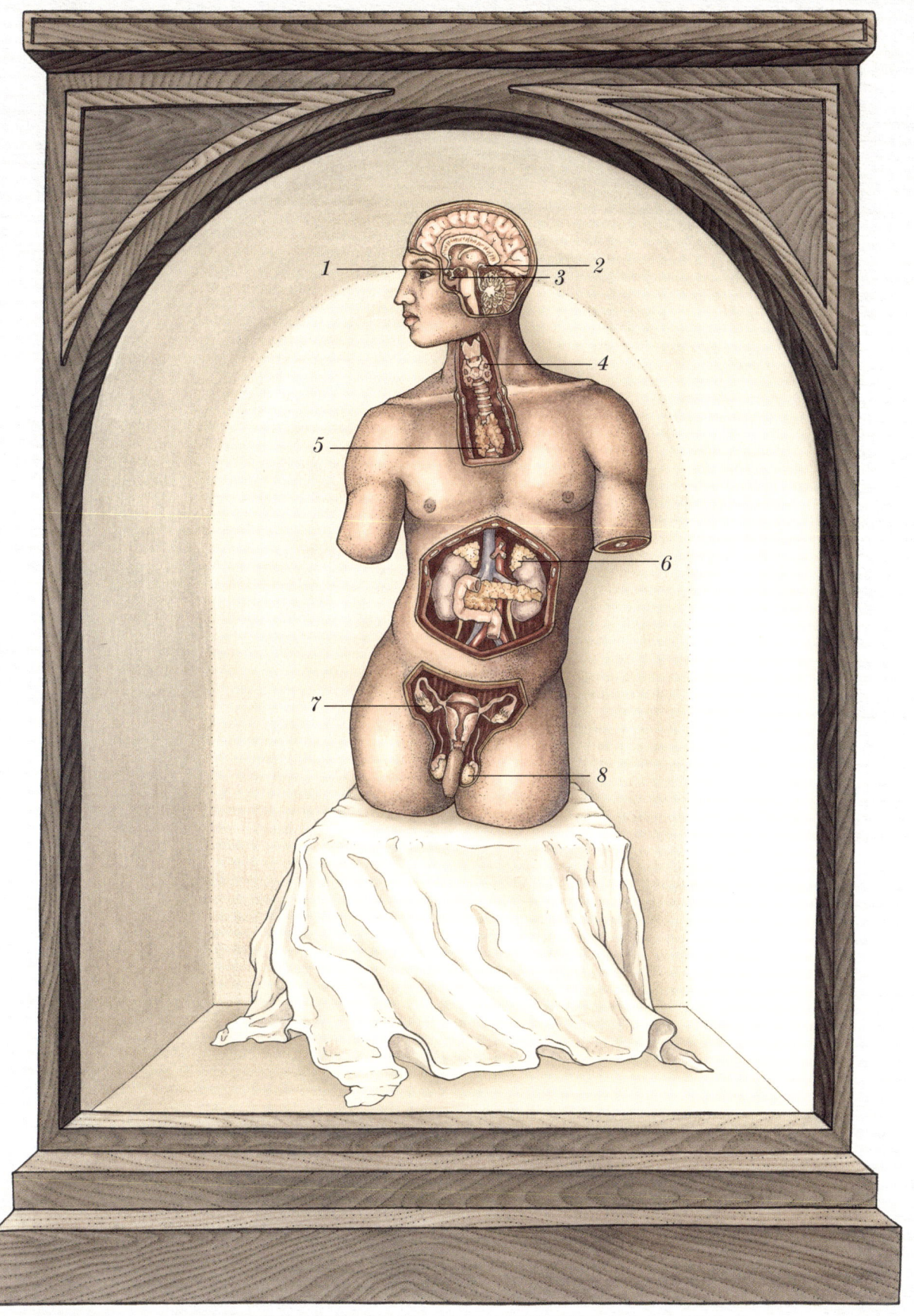

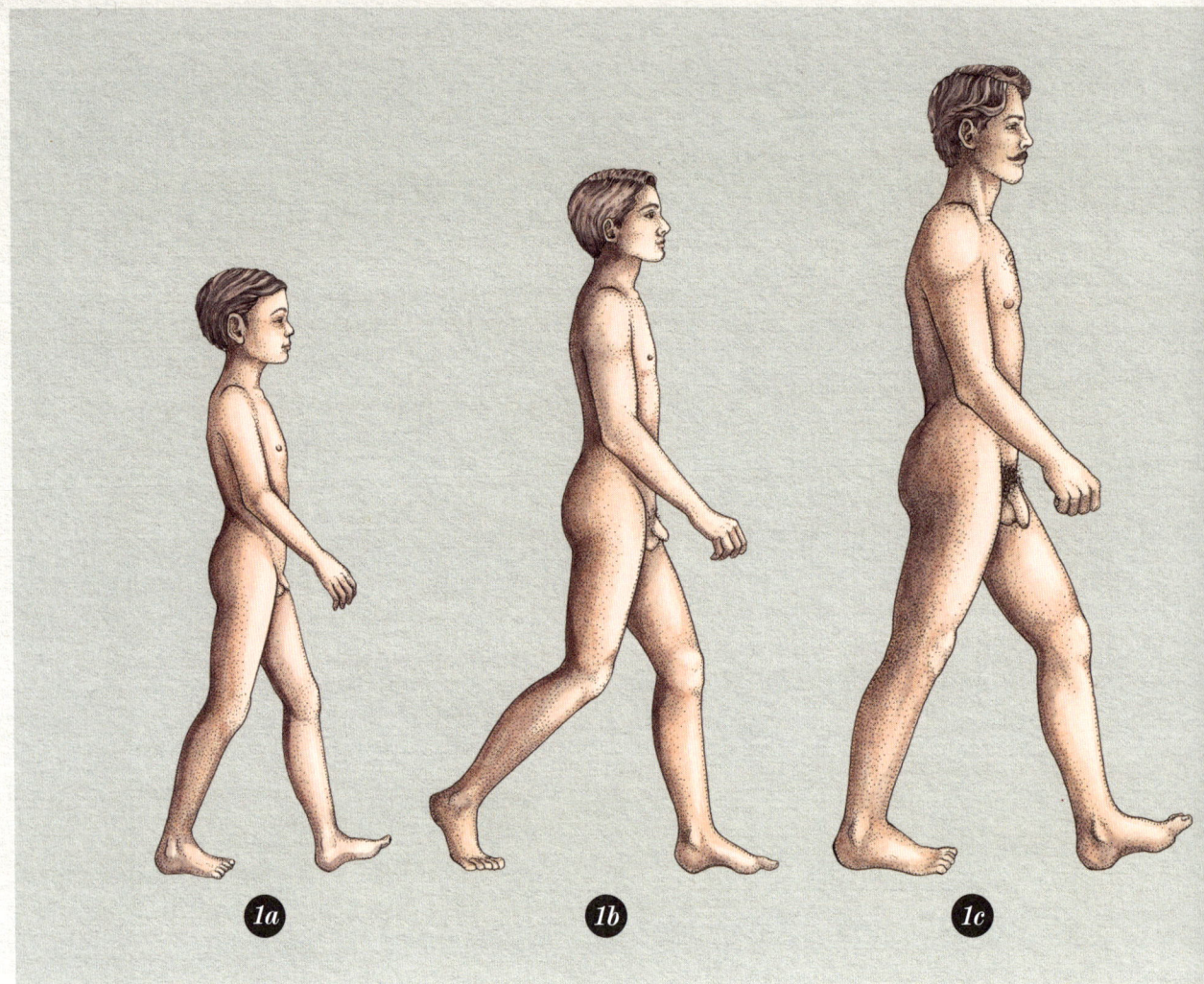

1a 1b 1c

THE ENDOCRINE & REPRODUCTIVE SYSTEMS

Puberty

The human body goes through huge changes in growth, appearance and feeling from childhood to adulthood. This transition begins at any time between age eight and age 14. It is called puberty and is triggered by an increase in hormones.

Puberty begins when a part of the brain called the hypothalamus triggers the production of hormones by another part, the pituitary gland. One of these hormones is a chemical that makes bones grow in size and causes 'growth spurts' in children. Other hormones stimulate hair growth in boys and girls. Sex hormones – oestrogen in girls and testosterone in boys – are produced by the reproductive organs and cause these organs to develop into their mature

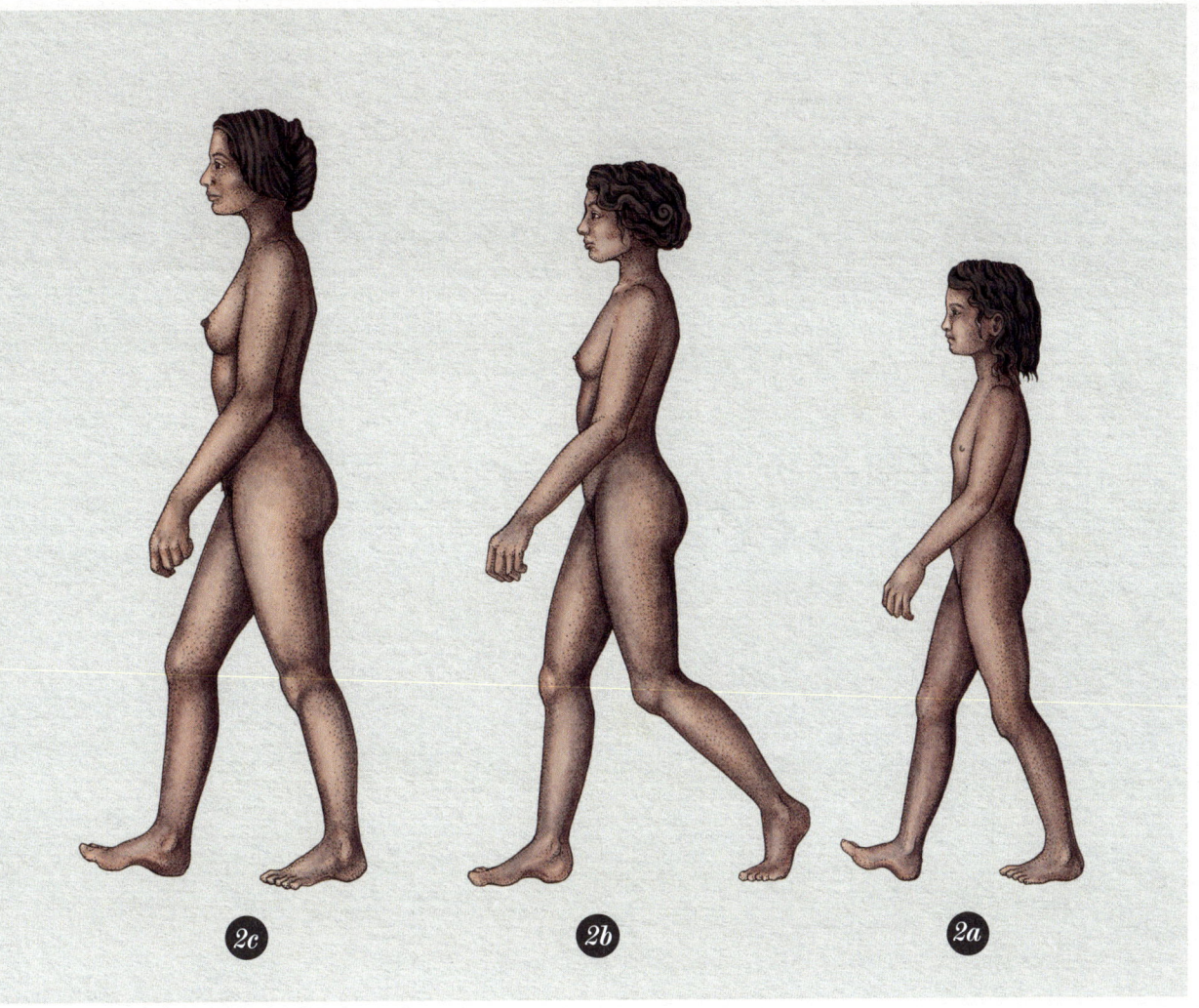

forms (see pages 74–77). The increase in hormones also affects overall body shape, making the differences between males and females more obvious.

It also has an effect on emotional responses. Sudden mood swings are common and people will often begin to feel sexually attracted to each other.

Key to plate

1: Boy to man
a) Pre-pubescent boy: Body shape is similar to female.
b) 10–15 years old: During puberty, boys grow taller, their sex organs develop, body hair increases and voice deepens.
c) Adult body: After puberty, male bodies are typically taller and more muscular, with fully developed sex organs.

2: Girl to woman
a) Pre-pubescent girl: Body shape is similar to male.
b) 10–15 years old: During puberty, the menstrual cycle begins and female sex organs develop.
c) Adult body: After puberty, female bodies have fully developed breasts and sex organs, capable of carrying and feeding a baby.

> THE ENDOCRINE & REPRODUCTIVE SYSTEMS

Male Reproductive System

Reproduction is nature's way of making sure a population continues. It happens when male sex cells (sperm) and female sex cells (eggs) fuse together as a result of sexual intercourse. These two cells are the start of a whole new life.

The main job of the male reproductive system is to make sperm. Millions are produced each day once a male reaches puberty. During intercourse, sperm is released from two organs called testes and travels down the thin tube of the urethra to the end of the penis (the male sex organ). Along the way it mixes with other fluids to make a liquid called semen, which leaves the body quickly during an action called ejaculation.

Sperm are some of the smallest cells in the human body. Each one looks like a tadpole: it has a 'head' with all of its genetic information (the instructions that tell cells what to do and what to become) and a tail to propel it forwards. To fertilise an egg, a sperm has to swim all the way through the female reproductive system – the human equivalent of 10 kilometres. Up to 300 million sperm can be released at once, but after one sperm reaches the egg, a chemical reaction stops any other sperm getting in.

Key to plate

1: **Testes**
This is where sperm is produced. Testes sit within a sac of skin called the scrotum.

2: **Epididymis and ductus deferens**
These tubes connect the testes to the urethra. They transport sperm to the end of the penis.

3: **Seminal vesicles**
These produce fluid that nourish the sperm and make semen.

4: **Urethra**
This long tube travels through the penis and is the route for sperm and urine to leave the body.

5: **Penis**
Most of the time, the penis is soft, as it is made of a spongy tissue. During sexual intercourse, this tissue fills with blood and becomes stiff.

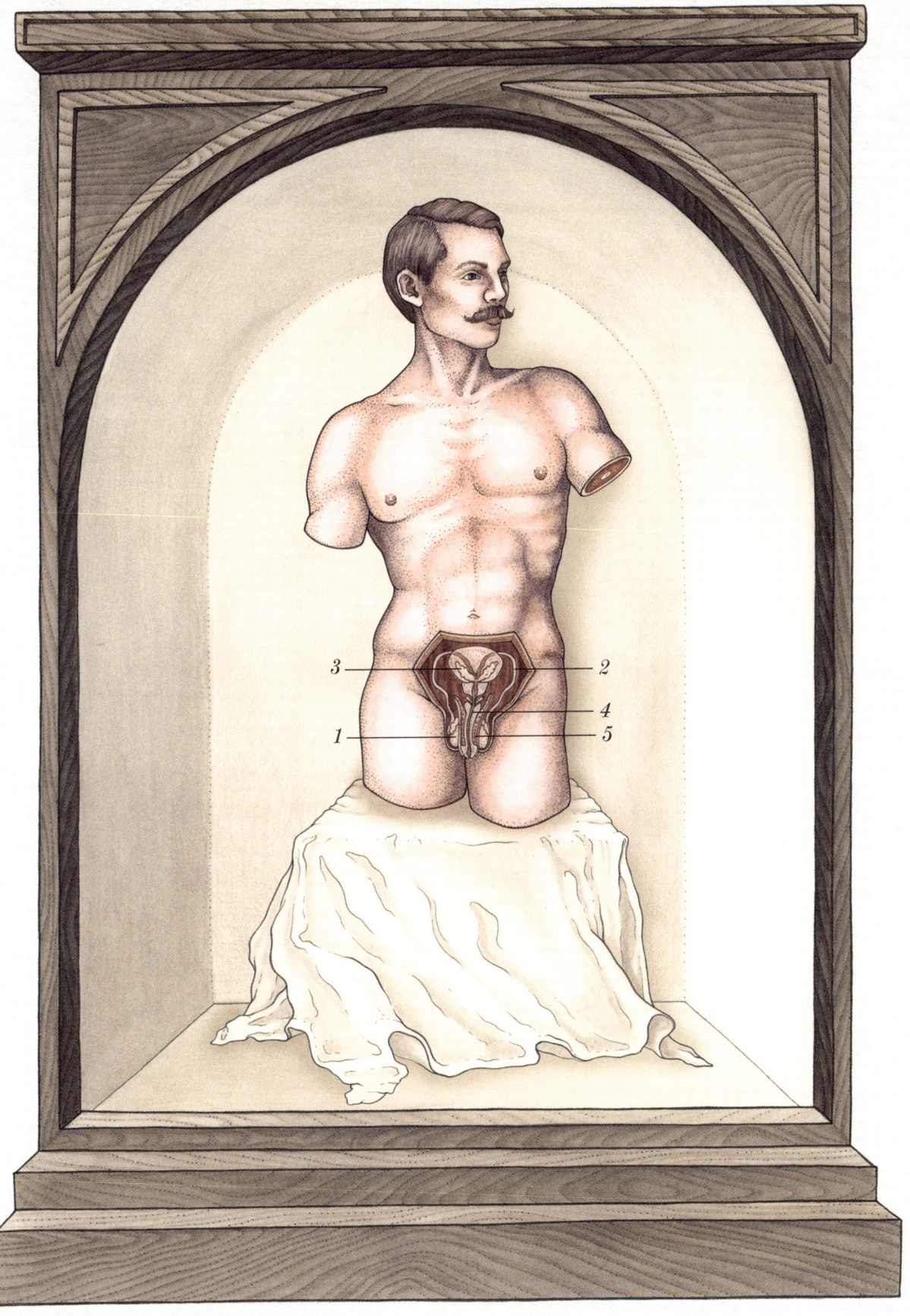

THE ENDOCRINE &
REPRODUCTIVE SYSTEMS

Female Reproductive System

The job of the female reproductive system is to produce female sex cells, called eggs, and to nourish, grow and protect a baby during pregnancy. Females are born with all the eggs they will ever have and cannot produce any more.

Two small rounded organs called ovaries produce eggs, as well as the female sex hormones oestrogen and progesterone. Once a female enters puberty, an egg will be released once a month as part of a process called the menstrual cycle. First, the egg will be caught at the end of the uterine tube, a passageway that connects each ovary to the uterus. Once in the uterine tube, the egg can be fertilised by a sperm. It then moves through the tube to the uterus, a muscular organ in the pelvis. If the egg has been fertilised, it lodges itself within the lining of the uterus and begins to grow. Special hormones signal to the body that the woman is pregnant, and other hormones to support the growth of the egg are released. If the egg is not fertilised the uterine lining is shed; a process called menstruation or 'periods'.

Key to plate

1: **Ovary**
Two ovaries sit in the female pelvis and produce eggs.

2: **Uterine tube**
These connect to the uterus, carrying the egg from the ovary. Fertilisation of the egg by male sperm often happens in the uterine tube.

3: **Uterus**
This is where a fertilised egg will develop into a baby.

4: **Cervix**
The boundary between vagina and uterus.

5: **Vagina**
This connects the uterus to the outer part of the female genitals. The external genitals (vulva) includes the labia (lips) and the clitoris. The vagina is the pathway for intercourse, menstruation and childbirth.

6: **Breast**
These produce milk for feeding a newborn baby.

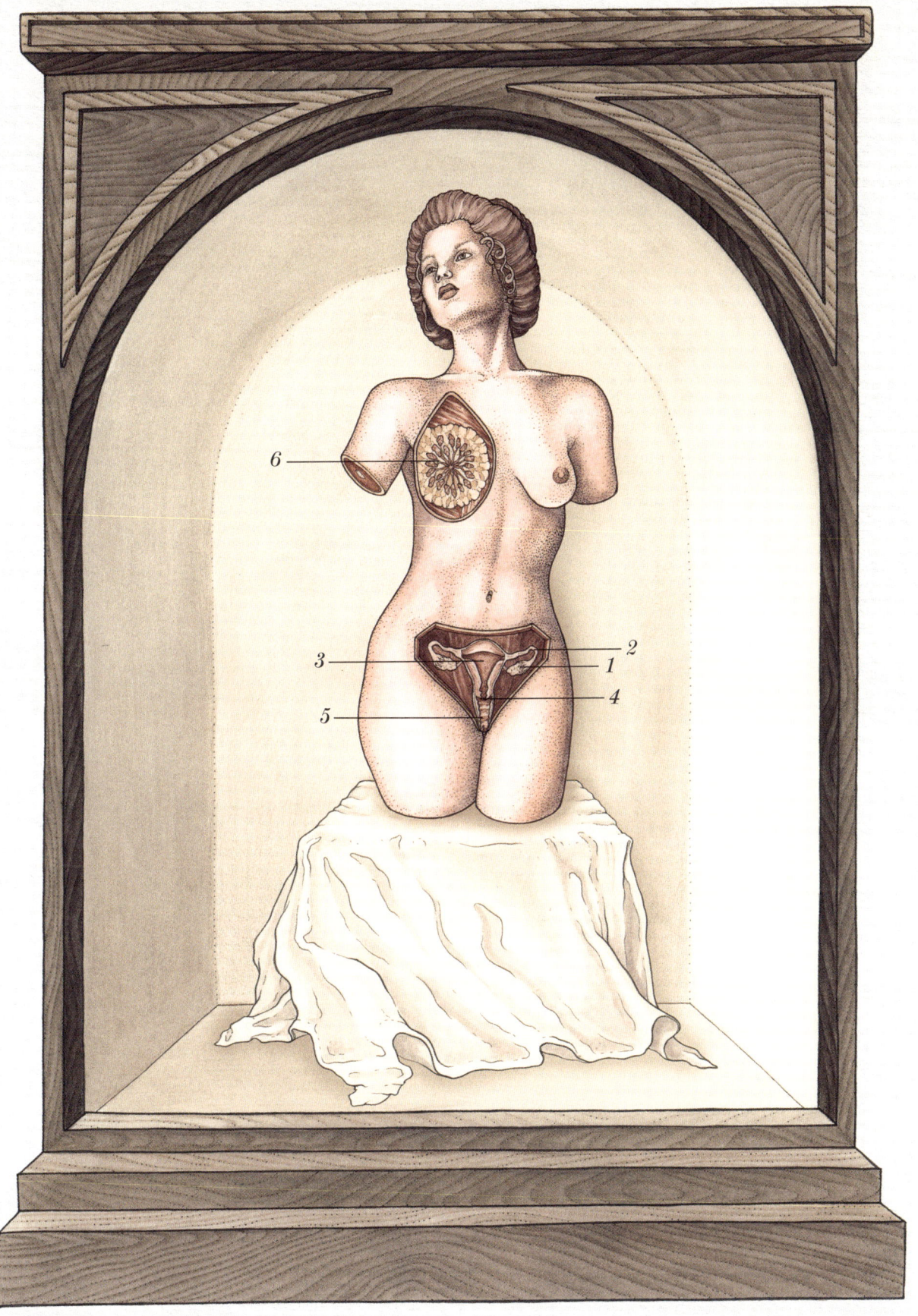

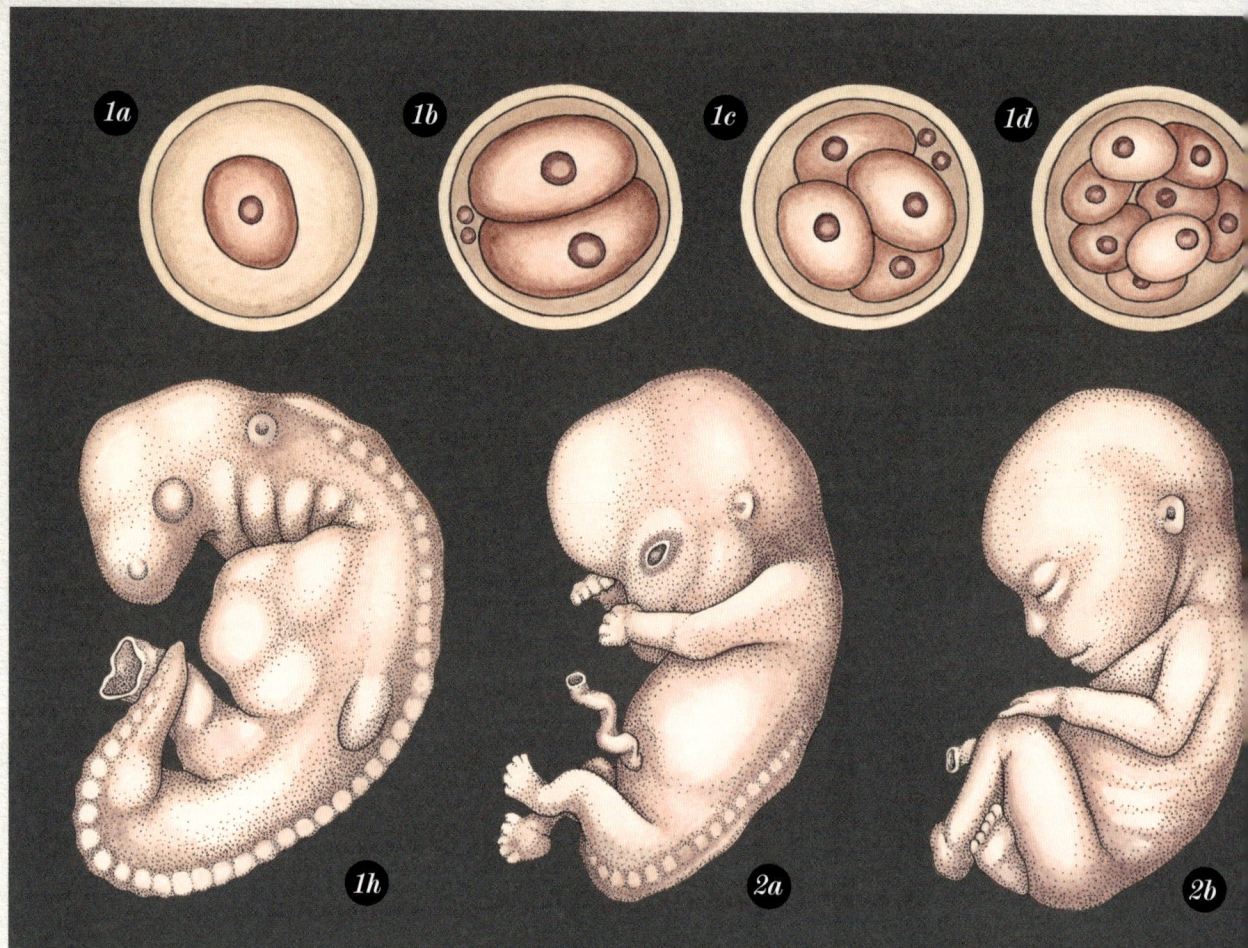

THE ENDOCRINE & REPRODUCTIVE SYSTEMS

Development of a Baby

Human life begins the moment a sperm fuses with an egg, a process called fertilisation. The genetic information from the mother and the father combine to make a whole new individual.

Once fertilised, the egg is called a zygote and will begin to divide until a ball of cells is made. This lodges itself into the lining of the mother's uterus. During pregnancy, the baby is surrounded by a sac of amniotic fluid, which keeps it safe. Nutrients and oxygen are passed from mother to baby from a round organ called a placenta that forms in the uterus during pregnancy. It connects

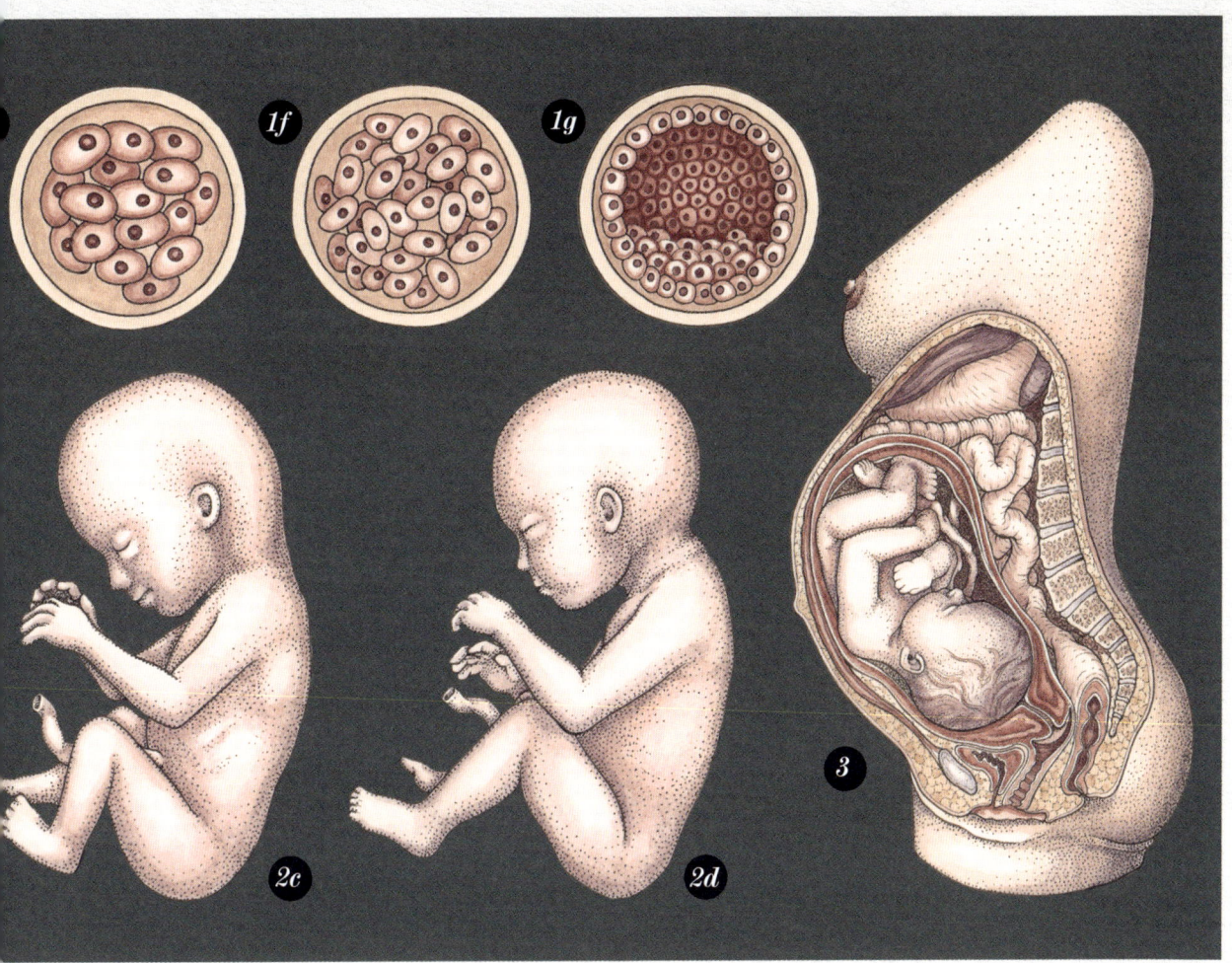

mother and baby with a fleshy structure called an umbilical cord.

By 20 weeks, the baby can begin to hear outside sounds and the mother can feel its movements. The average length of pregnancy is 40 weeks. When the baby is ready to be born, the muscles of the mother's uterus contract to prepare for pushing the baby out through the vagina. These contractions get more powerful, regular and painful until the baby is born.

Key to plate

1: Embryonic development
a-g) The fertilised egg (zygote) begins to divide into more cells to form an embryo. By day 5 or 6, the egg contains 64 cells and is ready to implant in the uterus.

h) End of week 4: The embryo has started to form.

2: Foetal development
a) Week 9 (2.5cm long)
b) Week 12 (5cm long)
c) Week 15 (10cm long)
d) Week 25 (34cm long)

3: Full-term baby
Between 38–40 weeks, the now fully developed baby is ready to be born.

Glossary

Anatomy The scientific study of structure and function of the body.

Appendicular skeleton Part of the skeleton relating to the limbs.

Arterioles Small blood vessels that carry oxygenated blood around the body.

Atria Two of the four chambers (areas) of the heart. They are usually smaller than ventricles, which are the other two chambers.

Axial skeleton Part of the skeleton relating to the bones of the head and the torso or trunk.

Capillaries The smallest of the blood vessels, where gas exchange of carbon dioxide and oxygen takes place.

Carbohydrate Large molecules that provide energy, often found in foodstuffs.

Carbon dioxide A waste gas that we exhale (breathe out).

Cell The smallest unit of life.

Contraction The movement of a muscle when it becomes shorter and tighter.

DNA Deoxyribonucleic acid: a molecule found inside cells that carries genetic information. This information tells an organism how to develop, live and reproduce.

Embryo An unborn baby that has been developing in the womb for less than eight weeks.

Endocrine function When a gland produces and releases substances into the bloodstream.

Energy The ability or power to make things change and move.

Enzymes Special chemicals that help certain processes in the body, such as breaking down fats and carbohydrates.

Excretion The process of getting rid of waste.

Exocrine function When a gland produces and releases substances into tissue.

Foetus An unborn baby that has been developing in the womb for more than eight weeks.

Friction A force that slows down movement.

Gland An organ that produce and releases substance into the body.

Glandular organ An organ made from glands,

Hormone A chemical that affects the body in some way and is produced by a gland and carried by the blood.

Molecules Groups of atoms (the smallest units of matter) joined together.

Mucus A sticky, slimy substance that coats, protects and moistens passages of the body.

Muscle A type of tissue containing long cells that can contract and create movement.

Nerve A bundle of fibres that passes electrical signals around the body.

Neutralise To bring something back to a 'normal' state.

Nutrients Substances important for healthy growth and development, often found in foodstuffs.

Organ A group of tissues that performs a specific function within a living organism.

Oxygen A gas we inhale (breathe in) and which we need to live.

Protein Large molecules that help to make up tissue, often found in foodstuffs.

Respiration The process of breathing. During respiration, we inhale (breathe in) oxygen and exhale (breathe out) carbon dioxide.

Tissue A group of similar cells that make up a particular structure, such as muscle, nervous or connective tissue.

Torso or **trunk** The body, excluding the head and limbs.

Valve A structure that stops fluid going in the wrong direction.

Ventricles Two of the four chambers (areas) of the heart. They are usually larger than atria, which are the other two chambers.

Venules Small blood vessels that carry deoxygenated blood around the body.

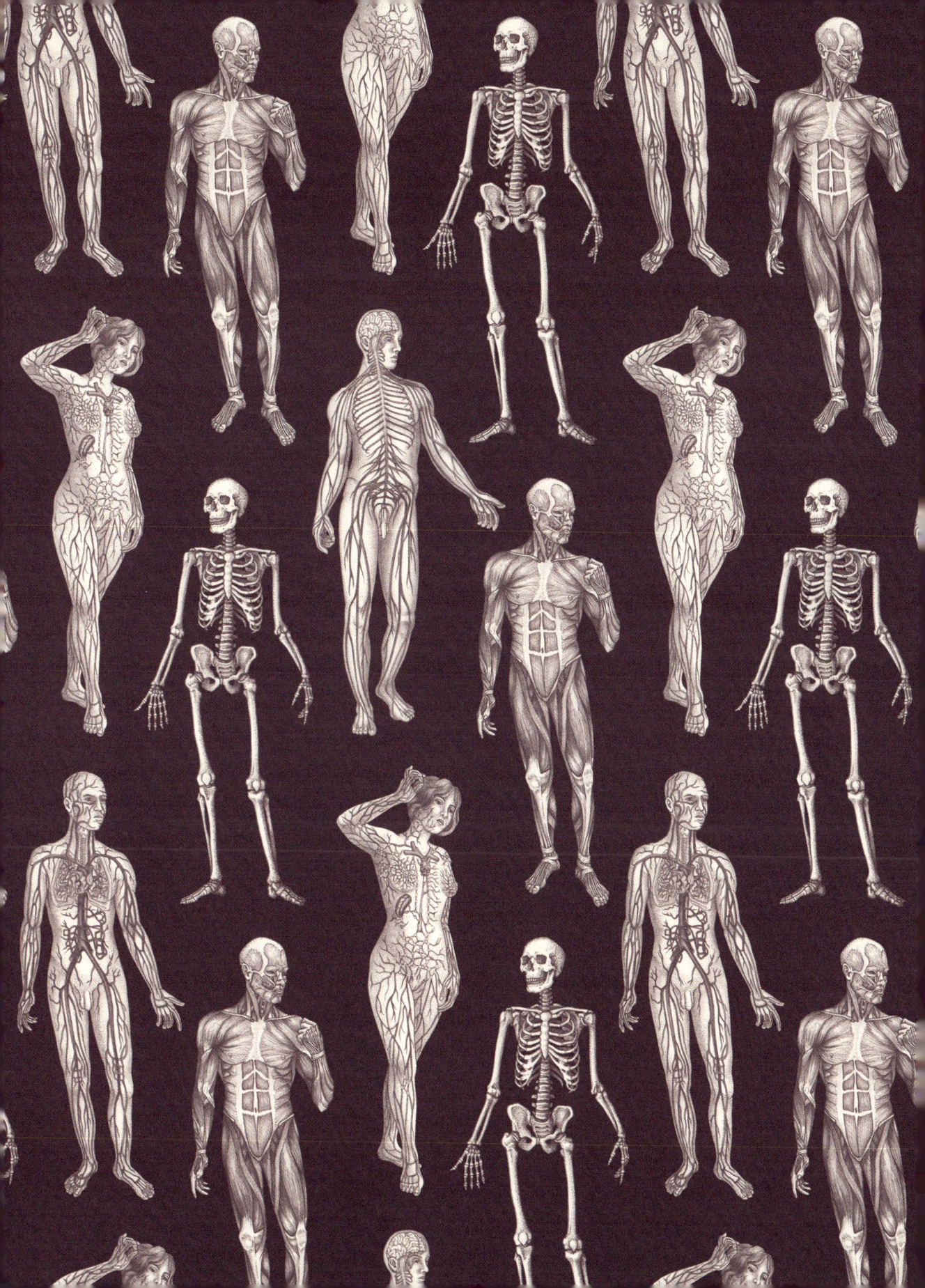

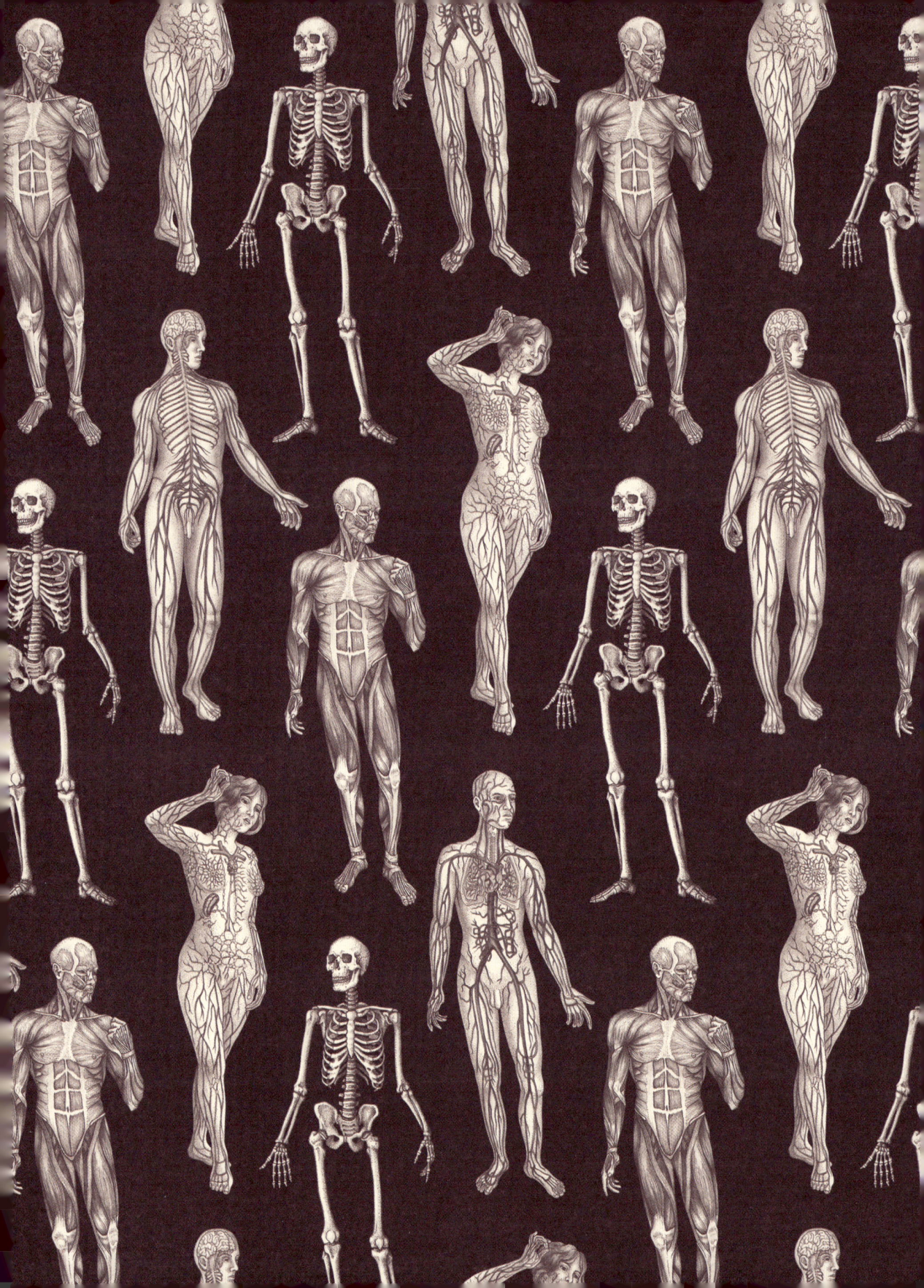